The LAMB *of* WALL STREET

The Lamb of Wall Street
How a Trailblazing Financial Executive Found Her True Calling in Creating
Economic Opportunity for Impoverished Communities Around the World

Published by Forefront Books.

Cover Design by Bruce Gore, Gore Studio Inc.
Interior Design by Bill Kersey, KerseyGraphics

Cover photo by Karen Bruton

ISBN: 978-1-63763-009-9
ISBN: 978-1-63763-010-5 (eBook)

The LAMB *of* WALL STREET

How a Trailblazing Financial Executive Found Her
True Calling in Creating Economic Opportunity for
Impoverished Communities Around the World

Karen Bruton

Forefront
BOOKS

DEDICATION

Ben and Ashley
Landon
Annalee
Lesley
Will
Sarah
Laura

ACKNOWLEDGMENTS

This book's story really starts from Paphos, Cyprus, where, after all the events of life, I had retreated and was contemplating what's next for my journey in this world. It was while I was sitting in that place by myself that I knew I heard a voice in my heart tell me to "tell the story now." I didn't really know what that meant, but after a couple of phone calls, I returned to Tennessee and thus began this incredible storytelling journey.

Honestly, I do not believe in looking back on my life. I tend to live in the current time and only look ahead; however, this book has forced me to remember my total life, and I am thankful for that.

First of all, I want to pay tribute to my father. He was just always Dad. To learn what he did in WWII forced me to look at him in a different way, not just as Dad but as a WWII hero. I now understand why I saw him on his knees every night praying.

To Gary Glover, who came up with the idea of this book. It certainly wasn't my idea!

To Michael Blanton, whom Gary called and spoke about my life. Michael, I did not know you, but I agreed to meet with you. I am thankful that I've gotten to know you and your wife, Paula, and will put you in my dear, dear friends' category.

To Wes Yoder, who has offered his expertise in writing and selling this book. I am so grateful to be working with you.

To Christopher, who has saved me in so many ways.

To Jim, whom I have known since my teenage years. He is my best friend.

To Travis Thrasher, who worked with me to tell my story. Travis, I thank God for you and what you have done for me.

To all the people whom I have met all over the world, you have changed my heart, you have changed my life. Whether or not I ever see you again, I will never forget you.

To Lloyd Shadrach, who is my friend and my teacher. He knew what to do that day I walked into his office. He stood in the back of his office while he told me to talk with Jesus.

To my Lord and Savior, Jesus Christ. I will follow you down this narrow path until I get to my final home.

TABLE *of* CONTENTS

Two roads diverged in a wood, and I—
I took the one less traveled by,
And that has made all the difference.

—ROBERT FROST (1916)

PROLOGUE

"*A*n option is not at all like a stock. It's a contract that has a beginning and an end. That's why they appealed to me in the first place."

In 2015, I sat in my office boardroom explaining trading derivatives to a couple of individuals from the SEC who had requested a meeting with me. I mainly traded derivatives, but I'll use the more common name of "options." Ever since deciding to trade with options back in 2003, I knew that a lot of people didn't understand how they worked.

"The pricing of an option is comprised of two pieces: intrinsic value and extrinsic value," I said as I began to describe how this worked. "So here's a simple way to look at options. If I buy a stock, I only make money one way, and that's if the market goes up. But with options, you buy or sell 'calls' and 'puts.' If I buy a call, I make money when the market goes up, but when I buy a put, I make money when the market goes down. I sell mainly puts."

Even though I looked at my way of trading as very simple, I realized people who are not familiar with derivatives do not fully grasp how this works . At the time, even though I wasn't trading under the SEC, I was still registered with them. I conducted all my trading under the authority of the CFTC (Commodity Futures Trading Commission) and the NFA (National Futures Association). These independent agencies regulated U.S. derivatives markets that included the options I was trading. I had just been through a comprehensive audit during which they didn't find any problems with my trading. The only thing they determined was that I was required to produce one more report for my investors. I already produced monthly reports explaining everything that was happening with their accounts; however, this was a report I had never heard of.

Since the recent CFTC audit hadn't found anything wrong with my bookkeeping and the way I traded, I wasn't worried about this meeting with the SEC. Even though I had just finished going through the process, I happily obliged them with their request to reproduce all the documents so they could conduct their own audit.

Less than a year later, I found myself meeting with the SEC again. This time, I was in a much larger conference room in their office in Atlanta surrounded by a lot more people . I was asked to speak into the microphone they placed in front of me. My lawyers, who were in the conference room with me, were told they were not allowed to speak.

There were two statements I won't ever forget from this meeting. As they kept asking me question after question, and I kept telling them exactly what I was doing, one man just threw up his arms and shook his head.

"Somebody else ask this woman a question," he said. "I can't get a straight answer out of her."

I was never asked about how I traded; they asked me what I did. The SEC never asked me if my investors understood what I was doing. My investors knew me personally and trusted me, and they loved it because they never lost a penny. But nobody at this meeting asked me questions about this.

I also remember a comment from someone from the SEC during a break: "We've got the female Bernie Madoff here."

(There was an irony about this particular meeting when two years later in 2018, two SEC codirectors were being interviewed by the House Financial Services Committee. As part of his response to the committee, one of the codirectors said that, "The CFTC regulates derivatives and commodities, the SEC focuses on securities.")

In a room surrounded by strangers who didn't understand how I traded—by SEC employees who didn't regulate what I traded—I wondered how I could be compared with the notorious man who died in federal prison after running the largest Ponzi scheme in history and defrauding thousands of investors of billions of dollars.

PROLOGUE

I had never intended for this trading thing to be something serious in the first place. The only reason I started this was because of a desire God put onto my heart. A desire to help others in impoverished countries all around the world.

My story—this story I'm sharing—isn't about the SEC. This is about how a girl from a small town in North Carolina found her true calling, and how an interest in trading helped fuel that passion.

15

"I have to face life with a newly found passion. I must rediscover the irresistible will to learn to live and to love."
—ANDREA BOCELLI, *THE MUSIC OF SILENCE: A MEMOIR* (2011)

Chapter One

FIND YOUR PASSION

WHAT ARE YOU MEANT
TO DO IN LIFE?

It started with a simple question. "What is your passion?"

I was sitting in the office of Dr. J. Howard Olds at Brentwood United Methodist Church when he asked me this. I'd recently moved to Brentwood, Tennessee, in 2003, and I knew I needed to find a new church. This was the first one I visited. I have always gone to a small country church, so on the first Sunday I attended Brentwood United, its size overwhelmed me. It had several thousand members, an organ donated by the late member Sarah Cannon (Minnie Pearl), and a choir and an organist who were amazing. As I sat in the back pew of the packed sanctuary, one thought came to my mind.

This isn't where I want to go. No way.

Then Howard Olds began to preach, and by the end of the sermon, my heart had been touched. He blew my mind. I knew I was already home. So shortly after that, I called his office and asked if I could meet with him.

"I've never been in a big church like this," I told him. "I wanted to visit other churches in the area, but I really appreciated your sermon. I just wanted to meet you."

When I first met Dr. Olds, we chatted for a few moments before he asked a question I couldn't exactly answer.

"What's your passion?"

I knew in my heart what he was asking me, but I didn't know how to reply. So I gave a simple answer.

"I enjoy music, art, and theater. Those are my passions."

The reverend had only known me for a handful of minutes, but he still chuckled and smiled at my answer.

"You know that's not what I'm asking."

He was right. Deep inside, I had felt God nudging me all of my life. There had been faint whispers and slight murmurs, all quiet suggestions that my life should have a greater purpose. But it's easy to let the noise of the world drown out those whispers. It's far too easy to let school, work, and relationships keep you distracted.

Over the course of many years, I had achieved a successful American life: college graduate, MBA, CPA, great job, and an easy street when I retired in several years. It all fit together so well. This could easily be my life's story. So why couldn't I answer his question?

"I don't know what my passion is," I said. "I want to find out what God is calling me to do."

"Has anything ever crossed your mind?" Dr. Olds asked.

"I'd like to take an international mission trip sometime."

As I learned later, you did not make a comment like that to Howard unless you were ready to follow through with action. Our conversation that day continued, but Dr. Olds didn't pressure me or ask any more questions. One week later, however, his secretary called.

"Dr. Olds said we've got a mission trip to Russia. He asked me to call you and tell you to join the team."

Almost immediately I said, "Okay, I'll do that."

I had been ignoring and running away from God's nudging for too long. I knew I had no more excuses. It was time to discover my true passion and calling in life.

I had no idea the journey I was about to go on.

When I picture my childhood, I see a kite flapping in the sky and horses galloping on the beach. These represent the power of possibility and the reward from creativity.

I can still hear that familiar question I would ask my father.

"Dad, it's windy outside. Can I fly a kite?"

"Sure. Go get me a newspaper."

When I recall my youth, I don't remember how poor we were. I didn't realize it at the time. I didn't know my father constructed homemade kites for us because he didn't have the money to buy them.

"Now go outside and get two limbs off that tree. Then go to the ragbag and bring me some rags."

I loved my father. My brother and I would stand next to him in the grassy lot next to our small house in Kannapolis, North Carolina, as we launched our homemade kites. Dad had crafted a frame from broomstraw and covered it with paper pasted together with a mix of flour and water. The kite tail came from the ragbag—usually an assortment of old T-shirts and torn pieces of bedsheets. Dad created the line by tying together different threads of leftover yarn he brought home from his job at the textile mill. He tethered the kite to strings from this large multicolored spool and unrolled it bit by bit as his creation took to the sky.

Once the kite was in the air, Dad let my brother, Larry, and me fly it, but even better than flying it was "sending a message" to the kite. Dad put a hole in a piece of paper and pulled the message through the line of yarn. There were no actual messages written on the piece of paper—the fun was in watching the wind slowly work the paper up the string, little by little, inch by inch. Sometimes it took half an hour to finally reach the kite, unless the paper got caught on the knots in the line. We were thrilled if the message got past the knots and made it all the way to the kite.

Dad got lots of practice making kites since most of them ended up eaten by the huge hickory tree at the back of our property, whose limbs took the kites hostage and where they stayed until they withered away.

My brother and I were baby boomer children born to a couple from the Greatest Generation. Our parents had married after serving during World War II. Our father, James T. Bruton Jr., spent four years overseas in the army infantry—his unit moved from Scotland, through England, across the Channel into Europe, and landed in North Africa. Our family had a picture of him stretched out on a beach with my mother's name, Ruth, spelled out in the sand in large capital letters. My mother was a nurse in the navy and was stationed in Jacksonville, Florida, where she tended to soldiers who had been ripped apart on the other side of the Atlantic. She didn't talk much about it, but I knew she had seen the worst of the worst.

Though they both left the military, the military didn't quite leave them. Dad ran the house like an army captain, and Mom was impeccably organized, her nurse's caps all starched and aligned on her dressing table, her uniforms perfectly pressed, her shoes shined. My mother was a collected, positive, and upbeat woman; she was also demanding and didn't accept excuses. She instilled in both my brother and me a drive to always be better. I didn't realize at the time how much I internalized her ethic. Looking back, I wish I could ask my parents more about their lives and how they were affected by what they witnessed during the war. As a girl, these two people were just Mom and Dad.

My parents never talked much about their jobs—I was rather oblivious to what they did at the time. I just saw them go to work and come home five days a week, alternating shifts so that one of them was always home to take care of us. For the longest time, Mom took the first shift and Dad took the second, which meant he was the one fixing our breakfasts and lunches for school. He made us oatmeal or grits and cinnamon toast, along with some bacon or fatback. Lunch was bologna or liver mush—a uniquely regional food made of pork scraps, liver, and cornmeal—usually with fried potatoes and canned corn or beans from the garden. Dad had a way of trying to be creative with his potatoes—one day he'd say they were home fries, the next day he called them French fries, another day they were German fries. But we weren't fooled—it was always the same thing.

Everything my father did meant something to me. I was crazy about him—he was a kind man and I was his little princess, and if I wasn't outside playing with my friends, I wanted to be around him all the time. Some of my happiest memories with my father were on our family vacations.

My father worked as a loom fixer in the weave room at Cannon Mills, one of the largest textile companies in the country at that time and the central industry of the city. He sheltered us from our family's economic hardships and figured out creative ways to take a family vacation in North Carolina. Cannon Mills shut down for two weeks every summer, so we would set out on adventures during that stretch of time.

It didn't matter that we couldn't afford to go anywhere and get a motel room. My father improvised.

One day he came home with a tent he'd bought. This is what we used when we traveled during those two weeks. We would sleep on the ground and think nothing of it as we explored North Carolina. The state is so diverse, with its rolling Smoky Mountains on one side and the sandy

Outer Banks on the other. Our primary destination became Cape Hatteras—a string of islands off the coast of North Carolina. Cape Hatteras was so remote that few others traveled there and the journey was part of the adventure—it took four different ferries to get to the island and then there were no roads, just one lane of steel mats on the sand—metal landing mats left over from World War II. If we encountered someone else on that strip of steel, one car had to back up to a side mat to let the other driver pass.

Dad drove a 1952 Pontiac in those days; it was two-toned green and had an Indian chieftain hood ornament that lit up when Dad turned on the headlights. Once we arrived at the Outer Banks, Dad let out air from the tires so he could drive short distances right on the sand. We set up our heavy canvas wall tent big enough for all four of us and camped right on the beach.

Cape Hatteras is known as the Graveyard of the Atlantic. Diamond Shoals, beyond the Cape, with its strong currents and shifting sandbars, makes the area a treacherous spot for ships to navigate. Thousands of boats, Spanish treasure ships, coastal steamers, gunboats, blockade runners, battleships, tankers, schooners, luxury liners, and more have met their demise near the Cape, and when we were little, we could see some of the shipwrecked debris coming out of the water. Larry and I often swam out and tried to pull off some of the barnacle-encrusted wood. A lighthouse stood on the Cape as a safety measure, a tall, tapered shaft with black-and-white stripes that curled like a barbershop pole. When we were little, it was left unlocked, and Larry and I raced up and down the steps, night or day, on its narrow, two-way staircase.

Another result of the innumerable shipwrecks over the centuries were the herds of wild horses that roamed the island, descendants of Spanish mustangs brought to the Americas five hundred years ago. Four or five horses would gallop past me as I sat on the beach. They'd eat the bushes, grass, and flowers from residents' yards. Eventually the National Park Service captured some of them and confined them behind fences, but a few wild horses still roam these beaches today.

It's amazing how the memories of your youth can later inform you of the lessons you didn't know you were learning. I look back on these makeshift kites and moving horses and see how my father was laying down pathways inside of me.

As a child, I didn't need an expensive toy. I didn't know how poor we were. All I knew was that my father loved me, and he wanted to spend time with me. As I've worked with kids all over the world from Nicaragua to Africa who can't even afford to buy clothes, I've seen a simple truth: children are children are children. They just want you to play with them. They don't want handouts. They want *you*.

My brother influenced me as well. Larry grew up with a great spirit of adventure in him. He explored the rivers and the mountains of North Carolina and would document and video the history of the places he visited. When I began to travel the world on trips to impoverished countries, it didn't bother me to sleep in mud huts or experience the wilderness. I was accustomed to these thanks to the adventurous vacations we took. I never thought I shouldn't be in some remote village sleeping on the floor. Instead, I was thankful for someone giving me a place to sleep that night.

Our lives are a series of preparations for what God has in store for us, but we first have to realize our purpose. Sometimes this comes at an early age. Sometimes this comes later in life. My moment arrived after I had built a successful career, after I had worked hard to build myself a comfortable existence. I didn't know the plans God had in store for me, and I couldn't imagine the adventures He would take me on. Little by little, God had been preparing me for these experiences, not just to serve in impoverished countries around the world but how to financially support this ministry.

On July 31, 2004, our team of seven arrived in Moscow with the goal of turning a bakery into a place of worship. I felt a great sense of calm arriving at the airport, knowing God was in charge. We would be working in the district of Perovo, but before traveling there, a little sightseeing in Moscow was in order.

It felt strange to be sitting in Moscow eating at the largest McDonald's in the world. Growing up in North Carolina in the '50s and '60s, all I knew about Russia was that Russians were the enemy. I had been through drills in elementary school where we would get under our desks to protect ourselves in case the Russians dropped the big bomb on America. My uncle built a fallout shelter and stocked it with water and canned food so the family would have a place to survive the expected attack by the USSR.

We took a tour of the Kremlin, walking through the presidential palace (home of the current Russian president, Vladimir Putin) and saw the world's largest bell and largest cannon. Red Square is just outside the Kremlin wall. I reflected on pictures from WWII of Russian troops marching through the Square, tanks rolling, flags waving. The grandest building at one end of Red Square is Saint Basil's Cathedral—now a museum—a Russian Orthodox Church built from 1555–1561. With its many colorful domes shaped to represent a bonfire rising into the sky, it is an impressive structure.

Our team was led by our tour guide, Elena, and the interpreter, Katya. Our lodging in Perovo that week was a college dormitory whose students were out for the summer. The hot water was turned off on a schedule we didn't have, so we never knew when we would have to brave a cold shower. This was just many of the things I had to adjust to on my first mission trip.

The bakery our team worked on had been purchased by a small congregation that was meeting there for church services. It was part of a larger building and was now basically a shell with a concrete floor. Our tasks ahead of us consisted of building a chancel and altar area, constructing kneelers to go around the chancel area, removing some of the columns in the room, placing studs around the walls in preparation for hanging drywall, and knocking out bricks to put in an exterior door in the back wall. With no Home Depot available for supplies, we all knew we had a challenging week ahead of us.

It would be a week full of hard work, community, and seeing God at work. Many songs were sung and meals shared. With each passing day, the bakery was being transformed. The brick work was coming along nicely. Thirty-six spindles were painted, and foam rubber was cut for the cushions on the kneelers. I was given the task of sewing the fabric for the kneeling cushions. The sewing machine I worked on was built in 1950 and had a hand crank.

At the end of the week, we finished constructing and staining a large cross that would hang in the sanctuary. The kneelers were finished as was all the brickwork in the chancel area. We purchased a vacuum cleaner and cleaned up all our construction mess. Our team prepared for the service on Sunday.

As church members entered the building before the service, they smiled as they saw the beautiful transformation. The service began with the planting of two grapevines in pots placed in front of the altar. Our team then led the congregation in singing "Hallelujah." All of us had tears in our eyes. Each member took part in the service in some specific way. Susan started by reading Psalms 150. Bill and Keith both read scriptures. I played the piano while Kaye, Chris, and Susan sang "On Eagles' Wings." Chris led the congregation in the Lord's Prayer, and I led the group in the Apostles' Creed. Kaye preached. Then we had communion and for the first time the church members were able to kneel at the altar while they received communion.

Later in the day, many gifts were exchanged between the new American and Russian friends. A feast followed in the evening at one of the church member's home. Later, the team sat around a table in the lobby of the dorm and talked about anything and everything. No one wanted to go to bed—it was our last night together. Several church members showed up the next day to accompany us to the airport. And the next thing I knew, we were on the plane coming home. I was returning to a life that would never be the same.

In many ways, my life resembled that bare building that had been rebuilt to serve God. My spirit had been altered by this trip to Russia, my heart, revolutionized. I had found a passion far away from the pews of Brentwood United Methodist Church. My purpose now lay with people in need living in poor places around the world.

There was a new question I needed to answer.

Where will I go next?

A PASSION FOR NUMBERS

Sometimes you discover a passion by being curious. This is exactly how I began my other unlikely story, my journey into trading.

Right around 2000, when I turned fifty years old, I started thinking and planning for the future. I had worked for twenty years and had earned multiple degrees. At the time I had most of my savings in investments along with some liquid assets, with my money being managed by an advisor at Merrill Lynch. I decided to start learning the stock market so I could have a better way to support myself in retirement. Someone told me around this time, "No one is ever going to manage your money and watch your money as well as you will."

This rang true. I didn't feel as if I was making any progress; my investment values would go up and down, with asset values increasing and decreasing but never really changing. I was talking with a friend about starting a business together, so we both decided to attend an investing seminar. These two- to three-hour seminars were usually held in hotel ballrooms during the mornings, afternoons, and evenings. There was no calculated reason to go other than we wanted to learn more about investing. We started going to seminars all over the country on weekends and just loved it more and more.

I had always been a good student in school growing up, earning straight As with math as my favorite subject. In elementary school and junior high, math had been so simple, and by my freshman year in high school I was studying college-level algebra and whizzed through it. It just clicked for me. I was probably the only girl in my high school with the kinds of math strengths I had.

With my math background, numbers made a lot of sense to me when it came to investing. I didn't see them as dollars; I saw it as numbers.

One day at a seminar we were attending, the instructors introduced an advanced investing program. My friend was excited about learning more.

"Let's do this!" she said.

"Are you crazy?" I asked her.

The program cost $22,000. It was about the fundamentals of investing, learning all the basics. How to read a graph. How to perform an analysis.

Looking at balance sheets and income statements. Seeing the buying and selling costs.

All you have to do is look for three green arrows or three red arrows and you'll be rich!

I thought my friend had lost her mind, but she convinced me to take it with her. So we split the cost and signed up for the program.

This advanced program in trading consisted of four courses. The first focused on the market in general while the second introduced options and technical analysis. The last two courses covered Advanced Technical Analysis and Advanced Options. Each course contained six DVDs along with a course manual that went into extreme detail with lots of examples. I was assigned a "leader" from the sponsor who called me once a week and tested my knowledge on that week's lesson. I had to pass before I could move forward.

The four courses took around a year to complete. I took all of this very seriously and stayed focused on learning all the material. It was the basis for everything that followed. I don't know what made me work so hard at this. I can look back on it and easily say it's how God was leading me in my life.

Using trading, I have been able to place millions toward helping others in the world.

After I got involved with the courses, I became fascinated by all of it; I just had an insatiable hunger to learn more and more. My first account was opened in 2002 with an investment of $10,000. I went to a lot of seminars, traveling to different cities where they were being held, mainly on the weekends. Most were sponsored by Sheridan Options Mentoring; I have gotten to know Dan Sheridan very well since. I was still working a full-time job, so I traded at lunch and at night using the methods I'd been taught.

Little by little, as I was learning more and more, I started experimenting with ways that I felt were trading safely. Eventually, I developed the trading plan I use today.

From the very beginning I saw myself as a fundamental trader because of my math and business background. Having been a CPA in North Carolina, I knew how to analyze balance sheets, income statements, and annual reports, so I would do the same to research a company before investing in it. I began to purchase stocks and sometimes even sold some calls against the stocks I owned.

For me, the market was a mystery to solve, and the only way to do that was to use my math abilities utilizing numbers to solve puzzles. If I used my skills correctly, I could solve the puzzle and be rewarded with cash. If I did not solve the puzzle, I would lose cash. During all this time that I've traded in the market, it still remains just numbers to me. I have said many times that you will never be successful trading in the market if you are driven by fear or greed. I am driven by neither, so it keeps me from making mistakes motivated by emotion.

I spent the next decade mastering the art and science of trading. I had no idea about this at the time, but all the skills I'd acquired over the years in business and education would be crucial in the years ahead.

"Fear incites human action far more urgently than does the impressive weight of historical evidence."
—JEREMY SIEGEL, *STOCKS FOR THE LONG RUN 3RD EDITION, 2002*

Chapter Two

DON'T BE
DRIVEN BY FEAR

RADICALLY AVAILABLE

You might never know your greatest calling if you allow your fears to prevent it.

There's something deep inside of me that has always fought back against my own apprehensions and anxieties. In 1974, while living in Charlotte, North Carolina, in my early twenties, I decided to face one of these fears head on.

Jumping out of an airplane.

I've never had a fear of heights, but the thought of stepping out of a small plane without a door terrified me—enough to challenge myself to overcome this fear. Back then, there were no tandem jumps. You were on your own. I decided to go for it, training all day and jumping out of a plane at 4 p.m. in the afternoon. The wing attachment was in front of the opening where a door used to be, so I was told to step out onto a very small bar, hold the strut, and let go when my trainer slapped my side.

Unless you have jumped out of an airplane by yourself, you cannot imagine the fear of climbing out of your seat, moving onto the side, seeing how high you are in the sky, holding onto the wing strut with the air blast hitting you, and then just letting go . . .

This taught me to understand what true courage meant. As Nelson Mandela said, "I learned that courage was not the absence of fear, but the triumph over it. The brave man is not he who does not feel afraid, but he who conquers that fear."[1]

Years later, I would have to conquer another kind of fear: the fear of committing to something even if I felt God pushing me toward it.

When I first moved to Nashville from Charlotte, North Carolina, in January 1986, I was hired by a national company that had just opened up an office. I stayed there six months and thought I had made the worst mistake of my life by taking that job: in six months, I did not have a single day off. I gave them my resignation and thought I had destroyed my professional life. Thankfully I found a great position at a great company where I worked for twenty years.

In the fall of 2006, I was a vice president in that company when they decided to sell to a

---

1 Mandela, Nelson. *Long Walk to Freedom: The Autobiography of Nelson Mandela*. Boston: Back Bay Books, 1995.

private company. I was part of the team that went to all the meetings and worked out all the sales arrangements. After being automatically hired by the new company, which had its headquarters in Belgium, the management team gave me a two-year contract to sign that said I would stay at least that long. In January 2007, I announced I was leaving.

In September 2006, I joined a small study group at my church called Companions in Christ where I would be encouraged and challenged to take a deeper look at my faith. This year-long spiritual formation class met every week with twelve other people, all of whom are still my friends.

In early January 2007, this group was discussing what it meant to be radically available to God. The idea was that you have to give up everything for God, that you have to listen to what He is calling you to do. Somebody asked me what I thought about it.

"I'm going to be honest," I replied. "I can't say I can do that."

"Why not?"

"What if God sends me somewhere like Africa. I'm never going to Africa!"

Famous last words. The group still teases me about saying that.

Traveling with a team to Russia in 2004 was my first step in a journey I had undertaken, but I still held many reservations inside. My next two mission trips were to South Africa and India. When I declared I would never go to Africa, I wasn't referring to South Africa, which I viewed as a modern country. The first trip came in 2005 and was once again through Brentwood United Methodist Church. I visited several areas in South Africa, including visits to Durban, Pietermaritzburg, and Howick. I was also able to go to Mpophomeni, a native African area.

During the white rule of Africa, during the policy of racial segregation known as "apartheid," this community experienced a lot of suffering. In Mpophomeni, a woman told me that the "police" showed up one day at her home when her husband had walked out of their house. They grabbed him, put a tire over him, and set the tire on fire. He burned to death right in front of her. I went back to that area a few more times (I had become chair of the committee that handled such projects for the church) and got to know several ladies and the chief of that area. We built a brick church there that still is used today, not only as a church but as a school.

To this day, Cape Town is one of the most beautiful places I've been.

In November 2005, I traveled to Calcutta, India. I was the president of our local Rotary club, so we traveled there for a service project. I had encountered some poverty in Russia, but it didn't compare to the conditions in Calcutta. Thousands of people lived on the street. Sacred cows roamed the streets as skinny as rails, and monkeys jumped all over the place. Anytime I stepped out on the street, I was immediately surrounded by beggars and children clinging to my legs.

I remember going to the convent where Mother Teresa is buried. When the car pulled up to the curb, I had to walk across the sidewalk to get into the building. The moment I stepped out of the taxi, I was surrounded by beggars, pushing and clamoring for attention. Yet the moment my foot touched the entrance to the convent, everybody stopped. No one followed me to Mother Teresa's tomb.

Both of these trips opened up my heart to the needs of the poorest of the poor in our world, and they made me start to experience a powerful, undeniable feeling deep in my soul. I began to feel like I was supposed to take a new path in life, that it was time to actually take that leap of faith that had been at the heart of God's murmurs for so many years. It was time to commit my life—not just my vacations—to serving the world's poor. Yet I still hadn't fully surrendered to the thought of making this my life and going wherever I could be used. That's why I admitted to my church group that I just couldn't give everything over to the Lord. I didn't *want* to be radically available to Him.

God did not give up on me. Instead, He started touching my heart. Night after night, I felt Him calling to me, nudging my spirit and whispering into my soul. I knew what I was being called to do, where I was being called to go, but I tried to fight it.

I was giving into my greatest fears.

Do you know what statement Christ made in the Bible more than any other? "Don't be afraid." He told his disciples this not to protect them, but to allow them to lead the lives they needed to live.

Max Lucado talks about this in his aptly titled book, *Fearless*:

> *When safety becomes our god, we worship the risk-free life. Can the safety lover do anything great? Can the risk-averse accomplish noble deeds? For God? For others? No. The fear-filled cannot love deeply. Love is risky. They cannot give to the poor. Benevolence has no guarantee of return. The fear-filled cannot dream wildly. What if their dreams sputter and fall from the sky? The worship of safety emasculates greatness. No wonder Jesus wages such a war against fear.*[2]

I was waging my own war, refusing to let go. One night, I climbed out of bed at 3 a.m. and yelled in the darkness, "God, surely you don't expect me to quit my job! I have no way of supporting myself!"

There are times in our lives that are monumental, and this was one for me. I was considering leaving a great career and diving into something where I had no experience. I thought about what

2   Lucado, Max. *Fearless: Imagine Your Life Without Fear.* Nashville: Thomas Nelson Inc, 2009.

it meant to call myself a Christian, and I decided I could either exhibit the faith I had professed all my life, or retreat into a safe zone and live the rest of my life wondering, *What if?* I decided to go to the middle of the lake and jump.

After much prayer, I realized I could no longer ignore the unmistakable calling from God. I said this to God: "I'm going to go to the deep end of the pool, and I'm going to jump. And Lord, if you don't catch me, I'm going to drown. Because I can't swim."

Two days later, I submitted my resignation.

I had no idea what was going to happen to my life now. I had just signed a contract promising I wouldn't leave this company for two years. Now a month later I was leaving. I saw my lawyer before giving them my notice, and both of us fully expected that I would be sued. Yet when I submitted my resignation, I was surprised by my boss's reaction. I explained why I was leaving: about what God had put on my heart and what I was wanting to do.

"Of all the things that I could battle, Karen, I can't battle that."

I was grateful that he understood where I was coming from. Even though I hadn't been sued, I still pictured myself ending up living underneath a bridge in Nashville, begging for food. I just knew I was going to lose everything. But I couldn't say no to God.

I jumped. And you know what?

He caught me.

THEY'RE JUST NUMBERS

If I let fears drive me, I wouldn't have taken a leap of faith and left my job. I also would have stopped trading, especially after two cataclysmic events happened before I took that leap. It took moving past those two situations to allow me to pursue the plans God had in store for me.

When I first began to invest, I knew what my mindset needed to be: *The only way I'm going to learn how to trade is to do the work.*

If you think this is easy, you're wrong. If you do the work, you will learn and get better at it. Seminar after seminar gave me tools and information I could use. Since I was a CPA, I jumped on fundamental analysis, studying all I could learn about a company. Two of the companies I researched and took a chance on early in my learning process were Apple and Elan Pharmaceuticals. After investing in both for a year, unforeseeable circumstances in 2002 and 2003 caused the stocks to fall.

First came Elan Pharmaceuticals. I had invested a considerable amount in them due to the strength of the company and all the new drugs they were putting out. One morning I went on my computer and looked at Elan. I couldn't believe what I was seeing.

Oh, they must have a glitch in the computer system. This can't be right.

Overnight the stock had fallen through the floor. First, an Alzheimer's drug they came out with was causing a problem, and second, they were having an accounting scandal.

A year later, another similar situation happened with Apple. I had studied their balance sheets, income statements, and annual reports. I had also studied Steve Jobs. I did all my homework. Then one day, Steve Jobs announced he had cancer. My investment value plummeted. I got out of it and ended up taking a significant loss just as I had with Elan Pharmaceuticals.

Fear easily could have taken over.

Of course, even then I knew two of the most commonly used words in the stock market were *fear* and *greed*. Giving way to making decisions based on these emotions eventually has a severe impact on your portfolio. Warren Buffet's most memorable quote from a 1986 Berkshire Hathaway Chairman's Letter uses these words well, "Be fearful when others are greedy and be greedy only when others are fearful."

The Apple and Elan Pharmaceutical stocks suddenly dropping a year apart meant I lost money I couldn't afford to lose. The easiest thing for me to do would have been to give up, to run away from the investing world. I could have easily stayed inside the airplane, refusing to step out and face the daunting ground far below.

I decided to face my fears, to step out of the plane, to experience adventure. And I allowed these events to teach me a lesson. Ultimately, they taught me a lot of what *not* to do.

Just like realizing how I needed to rethink the effectiveness of the short-term mission trips, I knew I needed to change how I was trading.

"When you make bad decisions, you learn from that and move forward."
— Michael Jordan
speaking to ESPN, 2014

Chapter Three

LEARN FROM
YOUR MISTAKES

THE GIRL IN THE YELLOW DRESS

I spotted her in a wasteland, in the poorest country in Central America, in one of the most horrific places I had ever visited. On the outskirts of Managua, the capital city of Nicaragua, the largest open-air trash dump in the region spread out over four toxic miles. La Chureca was called one of the "20 Horrors of the Modern World" by the Spanish magazine *Interviú*. I stepped foot in this veritable hell on earth in May of 2007, and that's when I came across a little girl living there.

In the middle of the hundreds of acres of stench and scraps, I met a beautiful young soul named Suyen.

Four months earlier, I had quit my corporate job, and two months later I established Just Hope International. The nonprofit was one way I was able to help serve the poorest people in the world. I was making enough money through trading to pay my bills. The trip to Managua was my first venture with Just Hope International. After meeting a man working down there, I learned about La Chureca and thought I needed to experience something like that. I continued to ask the Lord the same questions:

What are you calling me to do? Where do you want me to serve?

I knew I needed to be available to go where God wanted me to go. So when I heard about a place where desperate people searched through a sea of garbage for something to eat and children used plastic as blankets when they slept, I realized this was the place I needed to go. *I can go to that trash dump and feed those children,* I thought, *providing one nutritious meal a day for them.*

La Chureca's origin dates back to a cataclysmic earthquake that hit Managua on December 23, 1972, killing an estimated ten thousand people and leaving a quarter-million displaced from the city. More than five hundred city blocks were leveled, and in the weeks that followed, rubble and waste from the city center were hauled out and disposed of in the area that became La Chureca. Survivors of the earthquake began rummaging through the piled-up remains of the city, and eventually many of them set up camp there until a permanent community emerged.

Nicaragua is a stunning landscape of volcanoes, majestic peaks, lush tropical forests, and exotic beaches, yet this didn't prevent a century of corruption and political instability as well as numerous natural disasters from leaving the country in shambles. As I flew into Managua, seeing the gray haze of smoke hovering for miles, I was filled with apprehension. An estimated three hundred families lived at La Chureca, accounting for more than a thousand poor people who earned a meager income scavenging and reselling recyclables. Thousands more visited the site daily to work. All day long, massive trucks arrived unloaded some of the 1,200 tons of garbage Managua produced daily.

La Chureca was an assault on the senses; the stench alone was enough to make me want to pass out. I could not believe what I was looking at when I arrived: a hundred acres of moldering piles of paper and cardboard, broken glass, scrap metal, soiled diapers, rotting food, ripped clothes, plastic bags in an array of colors, household and industrial chemicals, and even medical waste. Families lived in the midst of this in makeshift hovels constructed of cardboard and plastic sheeting and sheets of corrugated tin pulled from the garbage. When the rains came, many of these flimsy cardboard huts dissolved, and the residents returned to the mound in search of more materials to rebuild.

I had never seen anything like this.

Half of the people living in La Chureca were children under eighteen. There was sheer glee on their faces each time a garbage truck appeared, as if the driver were Santa Claus bringing a sleigh full of gifts. Children and adults alike both chased after the truck, hoping to be among the first to comb through the fresh haul with their makeshift rakes and harpoons in order to find food or clothing or anything that could be sold for recycling. They worked fast because the trash piles were eventually set on fire.

It was one thing to see the faces of starving children on television and flyers, but it didn't compare to standing next to them. Watching their mothers give them tubes or jars of glue to sniff to help their hunger subside. Seeing them sitting in the trash, looking drunk with their eyes rolling back in their heads. The little food they received wasn't nourishing. When I saw several children with copper-colored hair, I assumed they must be dying their jet-black locks as a fashion statement. I soon learned the discoloration was a result of malnutrition. Instead of vitamins and minerals what they got from their scavenged food and polluted water were worms, parasites, lead, and toxic compounds. Many of the trash pickers had lung disorders and skin rashes and a host of other illnesses—all the result of the environment around them.

I had shipped a truckload of freeze-dried food full of nutrients to a port in Managua. The idea came from a nonprofit called Feed My Starving Children in Minnesota that provided packages of rice fortified with soy protein and necessary nutrients. Though each meal cost less than twenty-five cents, the Minnesota group provided the meals for free; all I had to do was pay for the trucking and shipping to Nicaragua, which was then underwritten by my Rotary Club back home in Brentwood, Tennessee.

Some of the locals helped me set up the food distribution site inside a corrugated metal structure located at La Chureca. We set up huge pots over a fire, boiling water and making the rice as children lined up with blue plastic dishes to receive a share. The food was only for the children, and every day for a week we fed a meal to however many showed up, usually thirty to fifty at a time. Two of those children stood out to me.

One of those was a little girl who arrived wearing a dirty yellow party dress she pulled out of the trash. Suyen wore that dress every day. Her lovely face couldn't hide a look of despair. Her skinny frame and hopeless eyes broke my heart. I didn't know at the time that young girls like Suyen were in constant danger of sexual abuse and exploitation, and many women and girls ended up being trafficked or went into prostitution to survive.

Those early days after starting Just Hope International were an education about life. I learned a lot from my experiences in Managua. I stayed at a boarding house run by a couple from North Carolina who renovated an abandoned military training camp and turned it into a motel of sorts for tourists and missionaries to the area. The house was made of cinder block and didn't have air conditioning, yet it was a luxury for the families at the trash dump. Suyen ended up happily spending a few nights in the extra bed in my room, something I mistook for being a great gesture on my part. She wanted a rag doll that was for sale at a nearby outdoor shop, so I bought it for her. Not much money . . . no harm. She named the doll Francesca and didn't let the doll out of her hands for the last few days I was there, even sleeping with her arms wrapped around her at night.

The other child whom I will never forget was a beautiful little boy who showed up in a yellow T-shirt and blue jeans caked with mud up to his knees. His bare feet were the color of clay. One day after getting his food, he turned to me and said, "Thank you." I was holding my camera and snapped a picture of him—his big, brown eyes so full of light and gratitude. Every day this same little boy came to eat and thanked me for his meal.

On my last day in Managua, I was walking with Suyen when she spotted another little girl who lives on the streets. Without hesitating, Suyen ran over and handed her Francesca, her one possession. I had never witnessed anything so unselfish; it still brings tears to my eyes. I was thinking I was doing something special for Suyen, providing a room for a few days, some food, a doll. What I realized was that she did something special for me. She changed my life, exposing me to a depth of love I didn't know was possible.

At the end of the week, I went home feeling completely uplifted by the project. Feeding those precious kids made me feel like a million dollars—it filled my heart with so much joy. Back home in Tennessee, I climbed in my bed with clean sheets in my nice home with running water. I felt on top of the world.

The next morning, I woke up thinking of Suyen and that little boy. I pictured her yellow dress and his sweet face. My joy turned to dread when I had a terrible realization.

Those children are hungry again. Yeah, you fed them, but you didn't change a thing.

Yes, I helped provide nutritious meals to those children for a week and it felt wonderful, but I hadn't altered their lives for the better or given them what they really needed.

There has to be a better way.

My wheels started turning. There had to be a much better way, a more lasting and sustainable approach to battling poverty so that kids, families, and whole communities could be elevated out of hopeless pits such as La Chureca. What we did for those kids was merely a temporary relief. It was a Band-Aid placed over a gaping wound.

You can't change people's lives by giving them things, I realized.

People need a hand up, not a handout.

This new attitude and approach changed everything.

IF THE RED LINE CROSSES THE BLUE LINE

I had a similar change in course and direction after the losses I took with Apple and Elan Pharmaceuticals. The two worst events in my investing life took me down a totally different path.

There's a similar realization that I had after this. I did everything I was supposed to do. I studied and invested heavily in Apple and Elan Pharmaceuticals, but the bottom still fell out with each of those stocks. I could have stopped investing after taking such huge losses, but instead I learned from these mistakes. They made me stronger. Just like my experience in Nicaragua, I realized what *not* to do.

I was very grateful for everything I learned at the investing seminar, but I was learning a system. I wasn't being taught how to trade. I needed to find a safer way to trade, so I moved from being a fundamental trader to becoming a technical trader working with options. A fundamental trader studies company reports, balance sheets, income statements, and annual reports. Being a CPA previously and working in public accounting, I thought this was my strength. A technical trader, on the other hand, looks more at charts and patterns of price movement.

The method I had been using to trade focused on company-specific events, which determined which stock to buy and when to buy it. The new method of technical analysis involved pattern recognition on a price chart. Based on what these patterns showed, I determined the entry and exit points. I no longer had to be as concerned by the reason something was because the patterns on the charts were signals.

After the Apple and Elan debacles, I saw the problems with fundamental trading. I probably could have mixed the two types of trading more, but my math background drew me totally to technical trading. I gradually moved to 100 percent options.

At first, I did a little of both (stocks and options), but I kept making a better return with the options. An option is also a contract, and it has a beginning and an ending date. This appealed to me.

No one convinced me to make this change. As I said, I could have simply given up after the losses, but instead I learned from my mistakes. I also made the decision to move over to options based on everything I had learned in my studying and weekend seminars. I completely understood the difference between the two styles of trading.

Anyone who decides to get in the market and do their own trading will be sadly disappointed if they do not study and learn what they are doing beforehand. There is no "system" that works all the time. I have met many people who want to find the easy way to make money. They will buy someone's book and read advice such as, "If the red line crosses the blue line, sell." Then the person starts trading this way, without having a clue what they are doing, and is shocked when they lose a lot of money.

Success comes from studying, more studying, and still *more* studying. Then practicing, practicing, and more practicing. And realizing that sometimes after you make a mistake, you need to change the way you trade in order to be more effective.

I don't ever look at something and tell myself, *Oh, I failed at this* or *I can't do this*. No. What I've done is gotten closer to success.

Every time I failed, I learned something that made me a better trader.

I see people getting into this thinking it's going to be quick and easy. It's not quick and easy. It is difficult to make money. I have persevered and it has taken a lot of time.

You have to continue to study and learn about trading. It's like learning any craft—you have to know the ins and outs. You have to practice. You have to do whatever you have to do.

Every time something goes wrong, you have to analyze it. *Why did this happen? What did I do wrong? What can I do better next time?*

It's taken me years to become an "overnight success." It took building a solid foundation, learning from my mistakes, and then making the appropriate adjustments even if they were difficult to make.

"Champions don't do extraordinary things. They do ordinary things, but they do them without thinking, too fast for the other team to react. They follow the habits they've learned."
— CHARLES DUHIGG, *THE POWER OF HABIT: WHY WE DO WHAT WE DO IN LIFE AND BUSINESS* (2012)

Chapter Four

STUDY IT,
THEN MAKE
IT YOUR OWN

*T*he only way to experience an *aha* moment is to allow it to happen. It doesn't come from waiting on the sidelines or sitting in the stands; it arrives after stepping out and seeing the results of your actions. It is the result of discovering something new and fresh after spending time realizing something else is broken.

My *aha* took place high up in the mountains of Peru three months after my trip to Nicaragua. This was my second time in Peru, with my first taking place in 2006 when I stayed at a hotel in Ayacucho to meet some people and hear their stories. That's when I first met Vincente, a minister in Ayacucho with whom I connected through a missionary friend. For this trip, we traveled to the village of Anyana to deliver some very special cargo.

I could hear some of our cargo clucking behind me during our two-and-a-half-hour drive on a rocky and narrow dirt road. Our van was loaded with crates of chickens and guinea pigs that we would be giving to the townspeople. During the trip, Vincente told me more about the village we were visiting, set in the heart of the native Quechua population. Anyana was one of the many Quechua villages that was decimated by a Maoist terrorist group called the Shining Path during their twelve-year occupation from 1980 to 1992. During that reign of terror, the group slaughtered native people who didn't join their cause, eventually killing around 70,000 Quechua and displacing around 500,000 from their homes. By 2007, the Peruvian government had only started allowing people back into their villages to reclaim their destroyed homes and land, and to start the process of rebuilding.

I knew there was a personal satisfaction in helping others, but I was starting to think there had to be a better way. We've all heard the statement, "It's better to give than receive." Giving to someone in need is particularly uplifting. It makes us feel good and important. But I couldn't shake off an important question:

Is a free gift the best for the person on the receiving end?

When I started Just Hope International, I focused on food and water, providing these resources without any expectation of something in return. On this trip, however, we provided something different. In addition to the chickens and guinea pigs, we also would be supplying the people seed and fertilizer to help them as they rebuilt their village.

When we arrived at the Kachimayu River, I realized the van couldn't go any farther. The village, however, was on the opposite side of the river. *We're going to have to carry the chicks and guinea pigs across the water ourselves.*

"No American has ever gone over to that other side," someone told me.

As I carried a cardboard box marked with little breathing holes for the chicks inside, I began to make my way through the swift running water. After taking a few steps, I could feel how quickly the river was moving. The water soon reached over my knees. We placed the boxes on our heads, and I couldn't help thinking a scary thought, *If I slip, I'm going to fall and drown.*

Thankfully we safely arrived on the other side and began to walk up the hill. Right away villagers greeted us by throwing flower petals at our feet. Earlier in the day, they had gone out into the woods and picked flowers to shower us with. It felt as if the entire village was there to welcome us. Their smiling faces ushered us into this dilapidated house with its roof blown off. Inside they had lunch waiting for us.

Dear Lord, please let me survive whatever food they're going to be serving.

Our meal consisted of a soup made with chicken, carrots, potatoes, celery, and onions. As we sat on rocks or boards on the floor and warmed ourselves in their hospitality, I realized this was probably more food than anybody in the village would eat in a month.

After lunch, we went outside where all the villagers gathered around us and sang songs. Their poverty didn't prevent their voices from being filled with joy and celebration. After the songs, they presented us with flowers and hugged each of us. Then they lined up to receive a male and female pair of guinea pigs along with two chickens each. These will be their initial gifts, with the bags of seed and fertilizer arriving later.

This was the moment when I got it. When the lightbulb turned on.

We're giving them a hand up, not a handout, I thought. With the use of husbandry, these animals would quickly become a food source, and with a little time, an income generator. The seeds and fertilizer would be used by the villagers to start gardens and farms. I saw the potential trajectory of these gifts.

To make an impact that lasts, handouts aren't going to do it.

Peru was the place where I discovered that when people have the appropriate assistance, they have a better chance to escape poverty. When they have inappropriate assistance, the poverty will more likely continue. Something I came to learn was that when the long-term development of people is called for, handouts do more harm than good. If a community has lived in poverty for an extended time, handouts only keep them there.

I ended up seeing this village rebuild their homes and support themselves through their own labors and their farms of guinea pigs and chickens. This was the place where I understood the celebration of the human spirit. It comes when a person or a people can work to change their own destiny. The key in improving the lives of men, women, and children is to provide the training and opportunities necessary for them to earn an ongoing income.

I truly understood the power of hope.

Offering a hand up, rather than a handout, became central to Just Hope's philosophy.

THE SECRET SAUCE

Much like shifting my attitude and focus when it came to helping people in need, I also changed my direction with investing after the Apple and Elan failures. As I've said, I ended up moving 100 percent to working with options. But I didn't simply decide to make this change without any knowledge of what options are or any sound rationale on why I was doing this. There were two specific reasons why I stopped trading stocks.

First, it got me out of the guessing game of asking, *Is it going up or down*? I stopped playing the earnings game. I went strictly into options in stocks, then moved over to the indexes. Second, we could play more safely; at this point, we started strictly shorting premium. My strategy became very simple. It involved going into one area and remaining simple. I gave up technical studies and instead watched price and volume.

I always start by explaining options the following way. Let's say you rent a house from me. It's August and you come to me with a proposal. You say you don't know for sure, but you may want to purchase the house from me at the end of the year for a certain amount of money. I say I will give you that option to purchase my house, but you will have to pay me to guarantee I won't sell the house before the end of the year. The renter "buys" that option from me; I "sell" it to him and he has to pay me. At the end of the year, he either exercises the option or lets it expire. Either way, I've already made money. So the buyer of the option has the right to exercise it, while the seller of the option is obligated to sell it at a stated price.

Here's another way to explain it. An option is a contract that has a beginning and an end date. It's not at all like a stock. The pricing of an option is comprised of two pieces: intrinsic value and extrinsic value.

The intrinsic value is the value of the option at the date of expiration. Actually, intrinsic only has value if the option is "in the money." Extrinsic value is the value of the option as it reacts to what the market is doing. It represents the external factors such as time and volatility that influences the value of an option. Of course, extrinsic value goes away the day the option expires.

I was learning how to trade and what options were while I still had a full-time job as a vice president and corporate controller. This is the thing so many need to understand: you *have* to put in the work and the time in order to study and master something. During this time, I was going to seminars on the weekend. Of course, I'd be able to attend many more once I quit my job to start the nonprofit organization. I was also taking that lengthy course in trading, having to read through four or five books with weekly assignments as well as getting calls every week on a certain day and time by someone who tested me on that week's lesson. If I didn't pass, I had to do the week over. If I passed, I moved on to the next week's lesson.

When people ask me how I've done it, I've always said the same thing: There is no recipe for the secret sauce.

Learn your job. Learn what you're doing. And with trading, the most important thing is to learn what to do *when* you get in trouble. We can all just slap on trades and do the easy part. It's knowing what to do when you get in trouble. I lost a lot of money until I learned what I was doing and learned *what* to do when I got in trouble.

It took a lot of work, a lot of study, and a lot of doing things wrong. But the program I was learning and the seminars I took opened doors and piqued my curiosity to learn more.

I needed to adjust my strategies and my thinking.

I had to experience more failures than successes early on in order to learn from them.

The important thing in all of that was that I didn't give up.

"Never say never, because limits, like fears, are often just an illusion."

—Michael Jordan,
Basketball Hall of Fame
induction speech (2009)

Chapter Five

NEVER SAY NEVER

WE ALL HAVE CHOICES

Sometimes when we hear the word *never* directed at us, we can take that as a challenge. And sometimes, I believe, when God hears us say the same thing to Him, He challenges us.

I grew up hearing my parents tell me that they would never be able to afford to send me to college. They were too poor to send me to college, so every time I mentioned it, they said they were sorry but they did not have the money to send me. They just planned that I would find a local job somewhere after my high school graduation. I knew my parents could not afford to send me to college, but something deep inside of me motivated me to find a way. Something deep inside me said I needed to try for more. I'm not sure where this strength and belief came from, but I knew the truth.

The only way I'll get out of this town and have a future is if I go to college.

Like so many people in Kannapolis, my father worked at Cannon Mills, one of the largest textile companies in the country at the time and the central industry of that city. In those days, every set of towels and bedsheets purchased in our stores carried the Cannon label. J. W. Cannon had established Kannapolis, "the city of Cannon," at the beginning of the twentieth century, and Kannapolis became the largest unincorporated town in the state. At the height of the mill's operations, the company was the largest producer of textiles in the world and employed more than twenty thousand people. Kannapolis was in many ways a company town, and Cannon Mills owned all the homes in the city center as rental properties for workers. Our neighborhood wasn't mill-owned housing, but my father's brother lived in a mill house, and most of the people on our block worked at the mill.

When I was growing up, J. W.'s youngest son, Charlie Cannon, was head of the family business and he also owned the hospital where my mother worked as a nurse—Cabarrus Memorial Hospital in adjacent Concord. In those days, most women were housewives who stayed home with the kids. My mother was the only woman in our neighborhood who had a profession. She set an example I followed throughout my life.

We lived in a small white house in Kannapolis. Within those eight hundred square feet my brother and I shared a room while we were young, and when I got older, the dining room was converted so that I had a private space of my own. Larry and I were very different. Larry, who has passed away now, was two years older than me. He was mischievous, while I was the perfect little child. I was the straight-A student; he was the rabble-rouser. I strove for excellence; he hunted for trouble.

Though I never felt a sense of want while growing up, I did know there was more opportunity outside of Kannapolis—and getting a good education was my ticket to a life I couldn't even imagine yet. I worked hard throughout my school years. At Winecoff High School, home of the Blue Devils, I earned straight As, played basketball, and performed the glockenspiel with the marching band. As I've mentioned, math was by far my favorite subject, and I excelled in every math class I took, regardless of how challenging it was.

During my senior year, I went to see the guidance counselor who was helping my classmates get into college. I sat in her small office among the stacks of paper and shelves of books, anticipating her sage advice on how to choose a good university.

"You're so smart," she said, "You could be a teacher."

Her suggestion caught me off guard. "I don't want to be a teacher."

She leaned across her desk and looked at me with something akin to sympathy.

"But you're a girl. There are limits to what you can do. You could be a nurse—your mother is a nurse. If not nursing school, how about Kings College in Charlotte? You're so good with numbers, you would make a great secretary for a law firm."

I felt rather stunned. Never before this moment had I encountered a situation in which me being female was a limitation. Throughout my young life, I never thought in terms of rich/poor, white/ black, nor boy/girl. My environment just hadn't brought much attention to such issues. I was going to be salutatorian of my graduating class; the vale- dictorian was also another girl. Being smart wasn't something out of the ordinary, and being female wasn't a known hindrance.

"Those are my choices?"

"Yes, you just find yourself a good man, get a secretarial job, and you'll do very well."

You're saying I'm never going to be able to do anything else.

Needless to say, I wasn't happy with the options the guidance counselor had presented, so I chose instead to ignore her.

I wasn't getting much encouragement at home, either, more like adamant discouragement. Everyone around me seemed to be putting up walls— you can't do this, you'll never do that. My father couldn't stand the thought of me moving away. Dad had left school himself after eighth grade when his father died so that he could take care of his mother. He said I should go to the local business college, be the best secretary I could be, and stay right there. I could have done what everyone wanted me to do— gotten an apartment nearby and taken a secretarial job, but I wanted more. Something inside of me said I had to try for more, and I didn't even know where that came from. Remaining in Kannapolis never crossed my mind. Moving away was the only way I knew to move ahead in life.

Moving was my answer to someone telling me "never."

I knew the only way I'd ever have a future was if I went to college. I kept applying for scholarships and kept being told the same thing over and over: "These scholarships are for boys only. We never give them to girls."

Every time I was told that, it made me more determined. I eventually found a few scholarships, and got a loan and found a job. Those all paid for every penny that I spent on my education plus the costs of having to pay back the loans after I graduated from UNC. They also silenced all those *nevers* in my life. I went to the University of North Carolina in Chapel Hill, and to this day, my blood runs Carolina blue.

Of course, I've been guilty of saying the same thing in my own life. My most memorable "never," as I've noted, came when I began to meet with our church group in 2007 and God started to stir my heart in a new direction. I remember distinctly saying the word "never" out loud.

"What if God sends me somewhere like Africa. I'm never going to Africa!"

Those are words I've had to swallow and eat. But I'm glad, because when I did go to Africa, I fell in love with it. I've fallen in love with every country in every subsequent trip I've taken.

My first visit to Africa came in the very same year I said never. In September 2007, I embarked on a trip to Malawi, a country in southeastern Africa. A year before I started Just Hope, I received an email from a man I had never met who told me about an orphanage in Malawi that was in desperate need of clean water. I was not in a position to help at that time, but a year later, I looked up that old email, got a phone number for him, and called. He had not been able to find help with the water situation. I told him I would commit to drilling a well at the orphanage. From this first trip in 2007, and the stories and pictures that came out of that visit, I was able to raise money to drill eight water wells and complete several other successful projects. One of these involved installing a solar-powered pumping system into one of these wells, making it possible for people to grow food during Malawi's dry season, which often brought devastating droughts and severe food shortages.

The incredible people I met would still be strangers if I had continued to say never to going to Africa. The incredible places would have remained settings I could only imagine if I had refused to entertain the notion of traveling to Malawi.

Refusing others' *nevers* can place us in positions we shouldn't be in. Saying never to God, on the other hand, can prevent us from the blessings He has in store for us.

INVESTING FOR OTHERS

The same year I traveled to Nicaragua, Peru, and Malawi, I also embarked on a new venture with my trading. Once again, it was initially something I said I could never do. And once again, it proved to be a blessing from God, a very big blessing that would go on to bless others.

Near the end of 2007, someone I used to work with asked to get together for lunch. When we got together, he asked me what I was doing now that I had left my old job behind. So I told him all about setting up the nonprofit organization named Just Hope International and about my trips overseas. He was visibly surprised and also curious.

"How are you paying for all that?" he asked. "How are you paying your living expenses?"

So I told him about my adventures in trading, how I had started it as an income source while I worked with Just Hope. Now I was making enough money in the market to cover all the administrative expenses. Naturally he wanted to know how I was doing in the market.

"What sort of returns are you getting?"

When I told him how much, he raised his eyebrows and told me that was a lot more than he was earning with his investments.

"If you're making that kind of money, you need to trade for me," he said.

"No, no," I quickly answered. "I could never do something like that."

We talked about it for a while, but my answer didn't change. My colleague kept pressing, however, long after our lunch. He kept throwing things out there for me to see, ideas and offers, and I kept saying no.

"I can't. This is my focus."

Never say never.

After several months of prodding, he finally managed to persuade me to start trading for him. At the time, I was working out of my home, both with my nonprofit and trading. Sometimes I'd wake up at two in the morning thinking of something, so I would simply get out of bed, go into my office, and work the rest of the night. My colleague's offer was hard to turn down.

"I'll give you an office space if you trade for me."

He owned a lot of acreage and raised horses and cattle on a farm. Across the road from this farm was a housing subdivision, and a very large Baptist church at the corner of the street, which was a large intersection. He had built a house on a piece of his property from which he began to work out of and offered me office space. His home was on the opposite side of the property through a large wooded section. You couldn't see it from where he drove to work each day. The property was so large, he had to drive out to the road from his home, turn left, go about a block or two and turn left back into the driveway that led to his new office space.

Since I felt like my home had turned into an office, and I missed the ability to walk out of the office and come home and relax, I took him up on his offer.

"It's gotta be something small," I said about how much money I was comfortable to invest.

"Small" to this individual meant around $600,000, which to him was a nickel.

At the start of 2008, I began to start investing someone else's money as well as my own. Little did I know that the country was about to experience an economic meltdown.

It was never in my pathway to invest for someone else. I was investing my savings to pay the costs of running a nonprofit company. At first, I began to start trading some of this man's money. But little by little, I was being approached by friends and business associates to do some investing for them. I eventually opened an investing company and took on the responsibility of investing the money of my friends and business associates. I never advertised my investment business. The people who were interested, over time, came to me. I never advertised because that was not my driving factor. My number one goal was serving God and building my charity as I felt He called me to do.

"God has created each of us with a unique contribution to make to our world and our times. No other person has our same abilities, motivations, network of friends and relationships, perspectives, ideas, or experiences. When we, like misplaced puzzle pieces, fail to show up, the overall picture is diminished."

—RICHARD STEARNS,
THE HOLE IN OUR GOSPEL (2009)

Chapter Six

CONNECT WITH OTHERS

MOVE OFF YOUR SEAT

I saw the woman right before I left Malawi to head back home to Nashville. She was a mother standing in front of me holding her child who was visibly dying of starvation. The image stayed with me, as did a familiar Bible verse from the NIV:

"Therefore I tell you, do not worry about your life, what you will eat or drink; or about your body, what you will wear. Is not life more than food, and the body more than clothes?"

The words in Matthew 6 are well known. Yet I struggled to make sense of them when I arrived back home.

"Look at the birds of the air; they do not sow or reap or store away in barns, and yet your heavenly Father feeds them. Are you not much more valuable than they? Can any one of you by worrying add a single hour to your life?"

I felt powerless, weak and angry. I struggled with the seeming discrepancy between the words of God and the reality of death I witnessed in Malawi. Shortly after this, I heard a poignant church sermon on this very text that provided an answer:

"God sends YOU, and that's how he reconciles this verse and the pain we see in the world."

I came to a conclusion. I realized I couldn't save the world, but I could do something to change one person's life impacted by poverty.

As a little girl, I never knew how poor we were. My parents were hard workers but struggled to make ends meet. They managed a frugal household; we grew our own food and my mother made all of my clothes herself using a sewing machine. I grew up poor without realizing it—I never felt a want for things I didn't have. I didn't know it was unusual to receive only one gift at Christmas. It never occurred to me that we could have gone to a store and bought toys instead of building them. Our parents never spoke about money. The only indicator I remember was when my dad got very sick and had to go to the hospital for surgery; he ended up paying off the medical bill for the next six years. In that time and place, that's just the way things were for everybody in our community. We all lived in houses the same size, we all drove old cars, we all went to the same schools, and nearly everyone went to the same Methodist or Baptist churches. I never felt out of place because everyone around me was in the same social class.

The only poverty I truly remember in those days was an area of Kannapolis that was called Shantytown—the black neighborhood about a mile up the street from where we lived. My dad usually hired someone from Shantytown to help him till our backyard farm every spring. When my mom and I caught a bus to downtown Kannapolis, the bus didn't venture through the streets of Shantytown but instead made one stop at a rundown central building. If anyone in Shantytown wanted to go to town, they came to that spot, and then once they'd gotten on the bus, they went to the back and sat down.

"What do I have to do to sit in the back of the bus?" I asked my mom.

It seemed like a benefit, that only important people got to go to the back.

"That's okay, you just sit where you are," my mother told me.

Too often, that's exactly what we end up doing in our lives: we sit exactly where we are. The only way to grow as an individual is to move off your seat and connect with others, to go see the world through other people's eyes, to try and understand who they are, to walk the same road they're traveling down.

To me, poverty always meant a lack of material goods and food. But the world traveling I started to do through missionary and relief efforts taught me that true poverty was the lack of hope. Providing hope was something I could do.

I'll never know what happened to that woman in Malawi holding her starving child in her arms. I do know she forever impacted my heart just like many others.

On a trip to Lilongwe, the capital city of Malawi, I crossed paths with a man named Elijah. I meet him in 2008 as he stood near my living quarters alongside several paintings of his own beautiful landscapes and wildlife. I usually stayed in a missionary camp in Lilongwe that had large walls around it, making me feel safe while I was there. One day, Elijah heard I was there and asked the guard at the gate if I could see him. The guard told me he knew this man, that Elijah painted pictures to sell and support himself, and that he was a very nice man

"Certainly," I told the guard. "I will come to the gate and speak with him."

That was the beginning of a friendship I would never forget. When I saw Elijah, he smiled, imploring me to notice his work. First I noticed beautiful paintings full of color, then I discovered something truly remarkable.

The man had no hands.

Elijah told me later that when he was a child, he was caught stealing food. His punishment was swift and terrible: the police chopped off both of his hands at the wrist. I couldn't imagine the agony, both from the immediate pain and shock, and then from the long recovery over the months it must have taken for such traumatic wounds to heal. And finally, the realization that without hands, he couldn't work. Without work, how would he survive?

In time, Elijah learned how to hold a paintbrush using the stubs at the end of his arms, overcoming a severe disability and becoming a true artist.

One day Elijah came to me and explained that he couldn't bring me any more pictures because he had run out of paint. I asked him where he bought his painting supplies, so after he told me, I went there and purchased everything he needed, spending around $25. When I got back, Elijah asked me what my favorite African animal happened to be. I didn't even have to give this a second thought: it was the giraffe. Elijah didn't say anything specific about this, just telling me he was curious.

About a week later, Elijah brought me a picture he painted with two giraffes next to a lake, with one of them spreading out his legs and trying to get his neck down to the water. Elijah gave me this as a gift. The painting hangs over my fireplace. It's worth a million dollars to me.

On my next visit to Malawi, I commissioned Elijah to create nearly 20 paintings for me. Elijah's perseverance and determination to thrive despite the harsh blow dealt to him as a child inspired me then and inspires me now. Elijah encouraged me, as someone wanting to help, that the human spirit to survive is strong. I heard a call to use my resources to tap into that spirit in the places of the world where the world has not been kind.

Seeing is never enough. Witnessing poverty in other parts of the world won't make a difference in our lives if we don't act upon it. I was changed by working with people around the world who had almost no material possessions and who loved and appreciated me for no other reason than my being present.

In my experience, I learned that the people I had gone to "help" usually ended up helping me more.

FINDING OTHERS

When I started raising money for Just Hope International, one of my first commitments was that I would never take money from the people contributing to the charity to pay any administrative expenses. Since I volunteered to do work for charities, sometimes I was asked to use my CPA experience to look at their books along with helping out with other office duties. This allowed me to see what a charity would cost and how much had to be deducted from a contribution to keep the charity open and pay expenses. Charities have to pay office charges and employee salaries if they are not working with volunteers and working out of their homes. Even though I realized that, I knew I never wanted to spend any donations on my needs. I wasn't running an organization; I was following God's calling. I figured I would be doing this charity work for the rest of my life, but I could not imagine it growing the way it did. I made a promise that 100 percent of a donation would go 100 percent toward helping someone in need. I've kept that promise to this day and will never break it.

"You give me a dollar, and a dollar will go to help others," I told investors. "None of it will go in my pocket. None of it will pay office or administrative costs."

I'm proud to say we're still following that rule that began the very first day the nonprofit began. And the only way we've been able to is through God blessing my trading efforts.

When I left my comfortable career behind and committed myself, one way or another, to reorienting my efforts to serving the world's poor, I was surprised how this took the form of a new career in the financial market. My "hobby education" in trading ended up working in our capitalistic economy. Hours upon hours of learning this new skill, most of which was done after hours back while I was still working full-time, began to deliver some not-bad returns. Those returns allowed me to cover my personal living expenses and administrative costs for my international service projects. I never wanted to go this alone, however, and it was and still is my fervent desire to find others who agree with my approach to solving chronic poverty and who want to join with me. Through friends, family, and church contacts, our base of support grew.

When I started investing for others and having success, more and more people approached me about trading for them. I saw this was a way that God was answering my prayers. At one point I went to the man for whom I first began to invest and told him what was happening.

"I'm being approached by lots of people," I said. "Everybody from business friends to personal friends."

The way he and I set up our initial investments had been a private investment fund, but I knew that needed to change.

"I'm going to have to open up to the public. You either approve this or not."

I never solicited for investors, and I never advertised. The people who invested with me were all people who knew me or knew another investor who knew me.

So he approved it, and in March 2011, Hope Investments was founded. We started with a million dollars, and within a few years, that million ended up being a little over two hundred million dollars.

As I've explained, I traded options, which are contracts with beginning and ending dates, so they are not traded like a stock. Every month, I distributed the value to the investor of every option that was closed that month. If I moved an option forward to a future month or sold future options, that value was not distributed to the investor until that option was closed and the money was in their pocket. If anyone was leaving the fund in a current month, I would calculate the percentage of ownership of the fund. If it was more than a small amount, I would call the investor and say I was going to close the future positions for his or her account and include that in the distribution of funds.

Just Hope International is a 501(c)(3) organization that is run by a board of directors. I wanted to open a nonprofit where I could place much of the money I was earning in the fund and pay all the administrative costs for Just Hope International, so I created the Just Hope Foundation. Every month when I calculated what Hope Investments was going to make that month and how much would be coming to me, I transferred 50 percent to the JHF investment account in Hope Investments. The rest was used to pay office expenses and employee salaries; whatever was left went into my account.

God was using my abilities in trading to advance His kingdom in the world. I was honored and humbled to know the difference we were making.

"Maturity is many things.
It is the ability to base a judgment on
the big picture, the long haul."
—Ann Landers,
"Definition of Maturity"
in the *Chicago Tribune*, 1999

Chapter Seven

KEEP THE BIG PICTURE IN MIND

THE SMALL CASKET

Investing in lives and investing in the market require a similar approach. There are no shortcuts you can take. When you see an opportunity that doesn't mean that you will find instant success. Many times, success can take years. It demands patience and always keeping the big picture in the back of your mind. Sometimes you have to watch and wait for your moment to make a move.

Then again, sometimes the moment arrives unexpectedly and out of nowhere, such as the memorable one that occurred in Malawi.

Located in southeastern Africa, Malawi is a land-locked country between Mozambique, Zambia, and Tanzania. A third of the country is comprised of more than 11,000 square miles of Lake Malawi. As one of the most heavily populated and least developed countries in the world, Malawi contains people living in rural areas and an economy based on agriculture. The country depends on outside aid to help its development needs, but this had been decreasing since 2000.

During my visit to Malawi in 2008, I befriended a local woman who ended up in the hospital. When I visited her, I learned that she was there because her husband didn't like the meal she fixed him for dinner so he broke her leg. Seeing her up close in that bed and comprehending the pain she was in touched me deeply. I wanted to do something, anything. I wanted to do more.

A short time later, as I was walking down a dirt road in the village, another woman approached me, walking straight toward me and then dropping to her knees right in front of me. As she looked up, tears streamed from her eyes. She spoke frantically in her local language, and I had no idea what she was saying. Thankfully, someone from the village was nearby who could translate, so I called him over and he interpreted what she said.

"She's begging you to pray that her husband stops beating her," the man told me.

An angry thought came to my mind.

Take me to your husband!

Then I let it go, knowing I didn't need to do that. I couldn't immediately rush to do something, to interfere or provide some sort of assistance. Instead, I fell to my knees and put my arms around her, then I began to pray for her. Even though she didn't understand the words I spoke in English, she accepted them with tears still in her eyes. I didn't know what else I could do.

Moments like this touched me deeply and sowed seeds to help women like her. I felt a strong calling to help wives and mothers and daughters in situations like this, yet I also knew I needed to learn more and listen to their needs, and to figure out what I could do and how we might make an impact. One way I learned this was to *literally* walk alongside them.

While we were working on the well projects and before any of the wells were put in, I got to experience what the local women went through when retrieving water. I accompanied a group of ladies who walked thirty minutes to fill a small bucket of water to bring back to their village while each balanced a bucket on their heads. The photo on the cover of this book gives a great picture of this; it's a shot I took while I was behind the ladies. As we made this trip several times, we had fun carrying our buckets. I wanted them to laugh at me and with me, so I did whatever it took to generate smiles and giggles. It didn't take much since I couldn't take even two steps without dropping the bucket of water I was trying to balance on my head. The women laughed at my comical efforts. Of course, I finally gave up since I didn't want to drop the water and waste it, but not after we had a lot of fun together.

The need for clean water was obvious, and this prompted the work that Just Hope did in Malawi. It was an example of the slow and methodical approach that was needed. On that first trip, I led a team in drilling Just Hope's first water well. Over the course of two years between 2007 to 2009, we dug nine wells in remote villages in Malawi. Our final work in Malawi was installing a solar-powered pumping system to one of those wells, making it possible for people to grow food during Malawi's dry season, which often brought devastating droughts and severe food shortages.

When you're working on big-picture projects, you end up experiencing small, but life-changing moments throughout the process. One of the wells went into a school for orphaned children. I had been there several times and even got to play with the children some. I was touched to have such opportunities. I helped the women cook lunch for these children and even had two days where I served the children as they walked by. It was a place I came to love.

One day I took several toy bubble blowers along with bubble solution to the orphanage. When the children were all outside, I started blowing some bubbles, assuming they would be excited. It scared them to death! Who could imagine that? I gradually showed the children what I was doing, and little by little, they finally got into it and started blowing bubbles. This taught me never to assume that people in other countries would react the same way we do in America.

There were setbacks to the work we did, and they proved to be more lessons in my work with impoverished communities. Some of the wells were torn apart after I left. Men came and ripped the metal off them, selling these pieces. The water from the wells was a blessing; at the orphanage, they were so appreciative and took good care of it. The solar-powered pumping system was a marvel and the people who lived in the area were so grateful for it. In other villages, unfortunately, the results were not the same. Some weren't asking for wells. I came to discover that sometimes when the wells were torn apart or stopped working for some reason, the locals didn't repair them. They simply returned to walking to the river for water.

When working on these big-picture projects, you could never forget the reasons you were doing them. A little boy I met at the orphanage was one of my reminders. After becoming gravely sick, he needed to be taken to the hospital. I didn't know what he had but I do know that if he had been in the U.S., he would have received the proper medicine and recovered quickly. I visited the young boy several times in the hospital, watching him grow weaker and weaker until he died.

I knew outsiders were not allowed to go to a funeral, so I visited the chief of the village to ask permission to attend the boy's funeral. The chief granted it to me and let me know which village the boy lived in. When I heard the boy was just going to be buried in a hole dug in the ground, I told the villagers I would purchase a coffin. I went to an outdoor "shop" where coffins were handmade and purchased one for a child that cost fifteen dollars.

The entire funeral lasted throughout the day. I stepped inside one of the huts in the village and saw the women sitting on the floor wailing. The small casket rested in the middle of that hut, open for all to see. I sat down next to them and just listened. After the women wept for an hour, they left the hut and the men arrived and began to wail themselves.

After the time allowed for wailing was over, we all started walking to the burial site. The women walked in groups with their arms around one anothers' backs while continuing to wail. I had never been a part of a funeral like this; I was so grateful to be allowed to attend. When we reached the burial site, lots of people from the village sat on the ground waiting for the burial process. The coffin was lowered into the site as people sang songs. I sat with the others and watched.

I can still picture his innocent face. That little boy will stay in my heart forever.

WALKING AROUND WALLS

From the moment I graduated from the University of North Carolina at Chapel Hill with an undergraduate degree in mathematics, I set out to find my first job. It was the spring of 1971, and in the early 1970s, the economy had tanked and my employment prospects appeared dismal. I had no input or help from parents, faculty, or my peers. All my friends had scattered to the four winds. My daily routine included reading want ads in the newspaper and calling in hopes of securing an interview.

One of the interviews I booked was for a job at Wachovia Bank at their headquarters in Winston-Salem. I can't recall exactly what the position was, but I do remember that I was highly qualified for it. I walked into the office of the manager conducting the interview. He was sitting down and looked short and small compared to the large, dark wood desk that filled the space between us.

The manager and I made small talk for a bit and discussed the open position. I expected to be questioned about my skills and potential contributions to the company. He smoothed his tie as he leaned forward in his chair, looking me straight in the face.

"Now, we have this job we need filled and we need someone we can count on. When do you plan to get pregnant?"

I was speechless. In that instant, my face must have turned ten shades of red.

"I have no plans," I stammered.

I was fresh out of college and just starting my adult life. I was looking to launch a career. I couldn't understand why this was his line of questioning, but he continued.

"Well, we can't just hire some woman who ends up pregnant six months later, after we've invested time and energy into her."

I can't recall anything that happened after that moment. He had embarrassed the fool out of me. I was so mortified. As I walked out of that office, I felt one inch tall.

That interview was a rude awakening to a hard reality: *You're a woman—welcome to the working world.*

I was discouraged, but I wouldn't give up. What other choice did I have? I just kept plugging away, keeping the big picture in mind. Despite my long, hard fight not to be sent to secretarial school, I ended up taking a temporary job as a secretary at a law firm in Kannapolis—the very place my guidance counselor had suggested—just to make ends meet for a while. For someone who wanted nothing to do with the profession, I had great typing skills. I tested at one hundred words per minute. Though it was not what I intended to do with my life, I simply reminded myself that I was doing a favor for a hometown friend who was out on maternity leave.

After a couple of months, I got back to hunting for a proper start to my career. I had discovered that the corporate realm was truly a man's world, but my initiation into it had only just begun.

I realized a few things at the beginning of my career in business. I went in with the attitude that I would work as hard as I could, make sure I was doing an exceptional job, and the raises would just keep coming my way. Well ... that was naïve on my part. I was always a very quiet person, and when I was a kid, I was extremely shy. I had to overcome my quietness in a positive way. I read several books about how to be a more outspoken person, how to be more noticeable, but I wanted to do all of that in a positive way. I also knew I still looked like a college student. I wore casual business clothing and still had long, straight hair.

A few years later, one book changed everything for me. *Games Mother Never Taught You: Corporate Gamesmanship for Women* by Betty Lehan Harragan was that book. It changed my life, my career, and my attitude about the workplace.

First, I had my hair cut. Second, I shopped for business suits and business shoes. Instead of just looking like a girl, I changed into a businesswoman. Since I was usually the only woman participating in meetings, I would always be asked to keep notes, so I stopped walking into meetings with a notepad. When I was asked, I just responded by saying I didn't have a pad of paper and suggesting that "Bob" keep the notes. Eventually I was not asked to take notes anymore.

I found a job working with Duke Power, a public utility, in their IT department. A year into my time there, another critical event in my career occurred. I was training a new employee who had just graduated college and had been hired into our group. I was happy to be training this young man with no experience. One day by mistake, this new employee's check was placed on my desk. Oops! I didn't realize it was his, so when I looked at it, I was totally in shock. He was making a good bit more than me. I knew it wasn't his fault.

I decided to be brave and go to my manager's office. I explained that this check was accidentally put on my desk, then I asked why this person was making more than me. My manager's response was that he was a married man with no children yet, but he needed to be making more money than a woman in the same job. I could have responded several different ways—becoming angry, threatening a lawsuit, or going after the manager. But I didn't respond right away, instead choosing to go home and calm my emotions down before deciding how to approach this.

Something went off in my head after this. I needed to step up my career to the next level, to a professional level, but what was this going to be?

I can be a lawyer, or a doctor, or an engineer.

I did not want to be any of those, however. I considered my schooling and knew I was good at math. After considering how I could use that math background, my new goal was to become a Certified Public Accountant (CPA). I went back to night college, took the accounting courses I needed, and passed the Uniform Certified Public Accountant Examination, preparing to go into public accounting as the next step in my career.

After completing my studies, I left Duke Power for the CPA firm of Laventhol & Horwath. I ended up becoming the first professional woman who was not a secretary that the Charlotte office had ever hired. After completing two years with L&H, I received a call from Duke Power and was asked to come back, not only as a certified public accountant but this time in a management role. Ultimately, I would become a vice president at the company.

I knew I could have tried to fight back against the powers that be and made a case for why I deserved to earn just as much as the male employees around me. I could have complained about others having a bigger office or being closer to the president. There were many walls surrounding me early in my career, and I could have either kept busting my head to get through those walls or I could have tried to walk around them.

I chose to walk around those walls. That was my attitude.

Little by little by little, I started gaining respect because I never took people on and never went after others to prove them wrong. I looked at the big picture, and I realized the truth: *I'm going to lose an argument somewhere down the road.*

I chose to not have those arguments and instead tried to build relationships.

It's good to look down the road and know where you're going instead of getting angry at being stuck in traffic. Sooner or later, the road is going to open up for you, so you have to be ready.

*"Personal involvement offers the best
way to determine if our charitable
investments are being put to good use."*
— Robert D. Lupton,
*Toxic Charity: How Churches and Charities
Hurt Those They Help* (2011)

Chapter Eight

MAKE A DIFFERENCE

ONE STEP A T A TIME

I was back on the continent I once said I could never go to, in a country best known for white sand beaches, blood diamonds, and a brutal civil war. With Just Hope operating in many countries around the world, I wanted to extend into West Africa, and our time arrived in 2010 after an exciting opportunity came our way.

An opportunity to provide sanctuary and safety and ultimately, hope.

This opportunity was partnering with a nonprofit operating in Sierra Leone, West Africa. Just Hope had recently donated some of our resources to help open a children's center in the city of Freetown. They expected to house fifty to seventy-five orphans and also to educate them on-site. This was a similar program to what we had done in Malawi except in this case the children had been removed from refugee camps and were living permanently in their new home.

The current conditions in Sierra Leone went all the way back to the 1770s. The American War of Independence provided an opportunity for thousands of slaves to gain freedom by fighting for Britain. When the war ended, more than fifteen thousand ex-slaves made their way to London, where they suffered unemployment and poverty. In 1787, a group of philanthropists purchased fifty-two square kilometers of land in present-day Sierra Leone from a local chief for the purpose of founding a "Province of Freedom" for ex-slaves. This became Freetown, today's capital of Sierra Leone.

Sierra Leone was a country rich in diamonds but had been in the middle of the blood diamond trading scandal due to a vicious ten-year civil war, which ended in 2002 and left thousands homeless, orphaned, and maimed. Many had been living in refugee camps ever since, and their futures were very grim. The civil war garnered regular media coverage due to widespread atrocities committed by rebel soldiers, many of them not yet in their teens.

Just Hope International was partnering with another nonprofit to address the impact that the civil war had on children, particularly orphans. At that time, there were more than 350,000 orphans living in Sierra Leone, and fewer than 1,800 lived safely in care centers. This raised the question, where are the others? The conditions that most of these children were living in, whether in a refugee camp, with extended family members, or on the street, were deplorable.

My good friend Jen Diers and I visited a village on the coast of Freetown called Kroo Bay. It reminded me of the desolation I witnessed in La Chureca, Managua. This village was built on top of a garbage dump with a river full of refuse and debris running through it. The stench and living conditions were horrific. Several members of our team couldn't even look around or take pictures. Jen described the experience on Just Hope's blog:

As I sat in the meeting with the chief of the village, I could not even hear what he was saying. I could only focus on a young mother sitting just outside the building with her infant daughter. That mother held her daughter, wrapping her arms around her tightly. The baby looked up in her mother's eyes and the mother smiled. This young mother then realized I was watching her and when I smiled at her, both the baby and she smiled back at me. The mother was so proud of her baby. She must have been so thrilled as I just sat staring at her beautiful baby. And in that moment, I knew why God had brought me here. In that moment I realized what God meant when he told us that we are all His people.

You see this mother loves her child in the same way I love Kobe, Luke, and Faith. She must have the same hopes, dreams, and wants for this little girl. She wraps her arms around her baby the same way I will when I get home to Iowa. She smiles when her child looks into her eyes. And God loves her and her baby the same way He loves me.

For reasons I may never understand, this mother lives in this horrendous, inhumane place. She washes her baby in water that a pig has rummaged through. She lives in a shack that is flooded to waist-high during the raining season. She has no furniture, no toys, no diapers, no bottles, no food. And God gave me the means to help! I don't know why. I sometimes ask God, why me? It is easy to see a place like Kroo Bay and become completely overwhelmed. The problem is so vast. The suffering is so deep. But I now know that this suffering exists and I am choosing to do something about it. I am taking just a small step. I can't clean up all of Kroo Bay. I can't change the entire situation. But I can buy some pillows for some kids at an orphanage who don't have any right now. I can teach the staff how to dispense Children's Tylenol. I can ready the place in the event the orphaned children of Kroo Bay end up at the orphanage. I am choosing to obey my God and know that His plan will see me through. I have no idea of knowing if that mother saw God's love in me with my smile but I do know that I saw God in her!

Jen's words impacted me. They showed that each of us can do something.

I am choosing to do something about it.

I am taking just a small step.

I can't change the entire situation, but I can choose to obey my God and know that His plan will see me through.

A day later, we took part in an "intake" day. The children coming to the orphanage were processed through the Department of Social Welfare, a government agency much like what we have here in the States. There was a child in the Kissybrook area of Freetown who was brought to the attention of the department. His name was Sherriff (pronounced *Sharee*) Kamara, a six-year-old boy whose father had abandoned him before birth and whose mother had recently died. The social welfare department had been granted permission for the boy to be moved to the orphanage.

Kissybrook resembled so many other sections of Freetown: dirty, shanties, people without jobs who spent the day sitting in the heat. Sherriff lived with his grandmother in a twelve-foot by six-foot concrete-block room sandwiched in between all the other concrete-block buildings on a long, steep dirt street. There were no windows, and a mattress on the floor stretched from wall to wall. There were four people living in this room; it had been five before Sherriff's mother died. The grandmother couldn't read or write, so she put her thumbprint on the government papers releasing her grandchild to the orphanage. She wept as she stood there with her grandson, but said she knew this was the only way to give him a better life. Sherriff said goodbye to his friends who had gathered in the street around his house and left for his new home. When asked if he was ready to go, he nodded his head. His grandmother hid her face in her skirt as she wept for him.

When Sherriff reached the orphanage, all the children had heard there was a new boy arriving and came outside to greet him. Sherriff stood at the entry gate to his new home where he was surrounded by children saying hello. He was then taken upstairs, shown his new bunk bed, and given new clothes. Afterward he ate dinner with the other children.

This was a deeply emotional day for all the team. I had tears of joy and tears of grief for little Sherriff, all at the same time. He would probably never see his friends from Kissybrook again. But I knew he had a chance now, that he was going against the statistics, that he would be safe and loved. He was also looking forward to going to school. His life changed that day and so did mine.

Once again, the history and needs of a place in this world become visible and personal. Proverbs 24:12 spoke to me during this trip:

"Don't excuse yourself by saying, 'Look, we didn't know.' For God understands all hearts, and he sees you. He who guards your soul knows you knew. He will repay all people as their actions deserve." (NLT)

I saw the sick children and the malnourished families. I watched the children not being cared for run to us and cling to me when we arrived. I felt their overwhelming need to be held, to have someone care for them.

Now that I know, I am responsible to act.

That's exactly why I was there and what we were trying to do. A temporary building housed forty-six orphans at that time who were receiving the right kind of loving care children need. They were receiving medical attention, being fed a nutritious diet, going to school, and, most importantly, being loved. We planned to help to purchase land, build a home, and take care of as many children as we could rescue from the streets, refugee camps, and the abuse from people wanting to exploit them.

Build a home, not an orphanage.

We called it a home because once in our care, they would know they were loved and that they had a huge family. And that family would be the caregivers in Sierra Leone and all the supporters of Just Hope who were helping us on our journey.

We couldn't change everything, but each of us could do something. As Jen said, I was taking just a little step. That was why I left my comfortable career behind and committed myself to making an impact to serve the world's poor, little by little by little.

Can one person make a difference in the world? I truly believe they can. And I believe that person is always the one looking back at you in the mirror.

CHOOSE TO MAKE A DIFFERENCE

When I think about one person who made a difference in the world, I think of Rosa Parks. My childhood coincided with the Civil Rights movement. I was only six when, down in Montgomery, Alabama, Rosa Parks refused to give up her seat for a white man and move to the back of the bus. Segregation was just the way things were for Americans back then. The folks in Shantytown had their own barbershops and grocery stores. I never met any of the kids my age who lived there—they went to an all-black school. It wasn't until I was a junior that our high school integrated, but even then, only one black student was added to our ranks.

When my parents first bought the little white house Larry and I grew up in Kannapolis, North Carolina, it was on a dirt road called Pennsylvania Drive. Around the time I was born in March 1949, the road was paved, more houses had bloomed throughout the neighborhood, and our address was changed to Pennsylvania Avenue. Dad bought the lot next to ours so we'd have a little elbow room. We flew kites and played baseball there, and Dad planted a garden large enough that he needed a mule, a plow, and a set of hired hands to prep it for planting every year. Produce straight from Dad's garden—beans, corn, tomatoes, radishes—fed us during the warmer months, and what wasn't eaten fresh Mom canned and preserved for later. I ate everything Dad grew save for the tomatoes. Those I wouldn't touch.

One of our town's movie theaters, the Palace Theatre, was known as the "black theater," and though my black neighbors could patronize other cinemas, they had to sit in a separate section. My family went to the Gem Theatre on Saturdays and stayed all day watching cartoons such as *Tarzan* or Disney movies such as *Sleeping Beauty*. We sat downstairs, and the black patrons were relegated to the upstairs balcony. The Gem even had two water fountains, one for "whites" and one for "coloreds." Larry told me that he once snuck a drink from a "colored" water fountain because he thought maybe they had different water than we had—but he was shocked to discover that it was just regular water. The separate fountains made no sense to him after that.

Looking back, it's terrible to consider all this, but when I was a kid, it was just life. I had no concept that black people were any different from us, besides their skin color. My parents never spoke a disparaging word or said anything that would have taught me otherwise. Everyone in our community was so challenged just to live life day to day that no one talked about being black or being white. I wasn't aware of the struggles that were erupting all over the country in that era until we finally got our first television, and then I started seeing it for myself—like news footage of Alabama governor George Wallace standing in the doorway of the University of Alabama in a show of resistance against integration.

After the Civil Rights Act was enacted in 1964, I remember seeing the signs directing "coloreds" to the balcony coming down in the theater, but people tended to self-segregate out of habit— whether at the Gem or on the bus. Those who did venture into previously outlawed territory weren't harassed for doing so. I don't really think anyone in our community cared. We were a small town, and blacks and whites worked alongside one another at Cannon Mills.

Working together was something we did on that trip to Sierra Leone in 2010. By the end of the trip, I discovered the needs in the country were overwhelming.

Its story was old and well known. This country was certainly one of the poorest in the world. Here in Freetown, the population swelled during the civil war as people attempted to escape atrocities during which rebels mutilated their victims by amputating arms and legs with machetes. Many stayed in the capital after the war, and the rural-urban migration continued. People in the provinces still thought they were better off in the city, so they continued to send their children hoping for a better life for them. Unfortunately, the children ended up living in deplorable conditions.

On the last evening we were there, our team heard Quami tell his story. He told about the day he was walking down the street with a friend. They came face-to-face with a rebel known for his cruelty. Quami and his friend were captured and bound with their arms tied behind their backs so tightly that their elbows touched. They were taken inside a warehouse where they were put against a wall with two other men. Quami said he just started praying. The rebel left the building but shortly returned. Quami said for no reason, the rebel let him and his friend go. Quami believes the other two men were shot. Quami has dedicated his life to helping the children who were orphaned from the war; it is his way of giving back.

During the going-away celebration at the orphanage, the children danced and sang for us. The children also prayed for us and said goodbye, calling us by name. It was a joyous night, but I still left with a heavy heart. It was so hard to say goodbye. Our hope in this effort was to continue working to help orphans. We needed land, buildings, water, food, and economic opportunities.

The Methodist minister Trevor Hudson wrote, "I believe that of all the horrible sins that plague our life together, the most deadly is indifference."[3] In whatever way you choose with whomever you choose, please choose to make a difference.

One person can truly make a difference.

3   Hudson, Trevor. *Questions God Asks Us*. Nashville, Tennessee: Upper Room, 2008.

"Security is mostly a superstition. . . .
Life is either a daring adventure or nothing."
— HELEN KELLER, *THE OPEN DOOR* (1957)

Chapter Nine

TAKE CHANCES

MADONNA IN MANHATTAN

"Auntie Karen."

As I stood on the dock waiting for the boat to take me across the water to the airport, I saw Quami approaching me. He, like everybody else in Sierra Leone who knew me, called me Auntie Karen. Quami was involved in a lot of the things we were doing. I admired his hard work and his strong faith. As I greeted him, I could tell he was concerned.

"Madonna is pregnant," Quami whispered to me.

I met his wife one evening almost in passing back in 2012. We said hello to each other but did not have any meaningful conversation. Now a year later, he was asking about advice on what to do about the pregnancy. I didn't have to ask why. I knew their backstory, how Madonna had already been pregnant a few times and had always miscarried. Having children here in Sierra Leone was important; it was a rite of passage for couples. Quami had once heard about a single lady who had died giving premature birth at a local hospital, so he and his wife had visited the hospital, signed some papers, and brought the little boy home with them. The child was not fully developed and within a short amount of time, he died.

With my boat approaching, Quami knew he didn't have a long time to talk with me.

"Do you think I should send her to another country with better hospitals?" Quami asked.

"Let me think about the situation and get back to you as soon as possible," I said as I stepped on the boat to leave.

When I arrived back in Nashville, I called an obstetrician, asking him for any suggestions on what might be done for Quami and Madonna. Almost immediately, he told me he would take care of her for free. My heart was deeply touched; I never expected that sort of response. After calling Quami and telling him what happened, he was very grateful as well.

The next hurdle was getting Madonna to Nashville. She didn't have a passport and had never flown. Since there was no way Quami could come, she ended up staying with me. I was able to raise the money for the plane trip. After Madonna got a passport, she stepped onto a plane for the first time in her life, all alone. She had to change planes in

Brussels and once more in Chicago before I met her at the Nashville airport.

In March 2013, I waited at the airport to pick up a lady I barely knew. A woman traveling for the first time by herself and flying far away from her continent all the way to America.

It turned out to be one of the greatest experiences of my life.

Madonna and I became fast friends and shared a lot with each other about our lives. I found it funny to have a woman who lived in Africa with no air conditioner in her house during the summer now living with someone who needed air conditioning. After working at my office during the day, I would come home in the afternoon to find Madonna wearing a sweater or a coat and her head wrapped up. She wore everything she could in order to be able to sit in an air-conditioned house. Even though I kept the temperature as high as I could tolerate it, she was still cold all the time.

Madonna took a chance to come to the United States and have her baby here. I took a chance to have her stay with me while this happened. For both of us, the outcome was amazing.

During her stay, I surprised her with a trip to New York in May. I had no idea what she would think of New York. I expected her to be scared in a big city like that, but it turned out to be just the opposite. She loved it. Madonna saw her first Broadway play, *Kinky Boots*, after which she met some of the actors in the play. As we walked down the street near several Broadway theaters, Bradley Cooper stepped out of a rear door in front of us. Madonna recognized the famous actor and went up to ask him for his autograph. Cooper was very nice to her, talking with her for a few moments while I watched in the background. I wanted her to have this experience.

Another surprise I had in store for Madonna was a concert at Madison Square Garden. Back in Sierra Leone, I had introduced her to the music of Andrea Bocelli, and like me she loved hearing him sing. I didn't tell her about the tickets I had to see Bocelli. I took her to a restaurant for dinner near the venue, and after we ate, we walked out to the sidewalk and I told her to close her eyes and just hold onto my arm. I guided her to the Garden, then told her to open her eyes. There, on the marquee in big letters, was the sign saying

Andrea Bocelli. She was so moved that night as she listened to him sing in person.

One day after coming home from work, I found her locked in her room upstairs. When I asked her what is wrong, Madonna told me she didn't want to come out.

"I've done something awful," she told me. "I'm so sorry for what I've done."

In my laundry room downstairs, I saw my ironing board resting with a burn mark in the cover where the iron had remained flat on the material, scalding it. This was why Madonna was so distraught. I went back upstairs and spoke with her through the door, assuring her that everything was okay and that this was nothing of value. Eventually she opened the door and calmed down.

The physician seeing her for no charge encouraged me to take and enroll her in the birthing classes being taught at the hospital. We decided to do the program together. There we were along with all the other husbands and wives! Both of us learned what childbirth would be like.

When the moment finally arrived, it came in the middle of the night. Madonna woke me up in the house and told me she was in labor. I drove her to the hospital and stayed with her through the entire birthing process. I treasured that time. I'm in awe of the miracle I witnessed.

The baby was named Karen. What an honor.

KAREN IN FIRENZE

I understood Madonna's apprehension at leaving her country and her world to go to a strange land and reside with a stranger before giving birth to her child. I took a similar trip in college, though for me it was simply an adventure and I wasn't pregnant.

As a kid, I had very little concept of the wider world. I didn't trace the lines on a map or spin a globe and dream about places I might go, and the only connection I had to life outside my Kannapolis community was from my brother's CB radio. Larry and I huddled around the silver and black box, microphone in hand, calling into the night: "Breaker, breaker this is KCI-5196." Usually we just ended up talking to our neighbor Ralph and his two kids across the street. But on a clear summer night when the conditions were right, we could shoot skip and talk to people farther away. Skip was what happened when the signals bounced off the ionosphere, and we never know where they might come down. Larry and I talked to people as far away as Ohio or Florida, and once we even reached a guy in Ontario, Canada. We sent our fellow radio operators QSL cards—postcards of sorts that identified our call signs. Our bedroom wall was plastered with these postcards, most from North Carolina but also a scattering from across the Eastern Seaboard.

By the time I attended the University of North Carolina, I started to learn more about the world. My second roommate at UNC, Johanna, born and raised in South Africa, helped this happen. During the two years I lived with her, Johanna was very influential in broadening my imagination and curiosity beyond the immediate borders that had framed my life up to then. She became one of my dearest friends.

The more I learned from Johanna, the more curious I became with life outside of North Carolina. Johanna was majoring in archaeology at Chapel Hill, and the subject interested me enough that I applied to be part of a dig in Winchester, the ancient capital of England, during the summer before my junior year. A number of sites were being excavated within the Winchester city limits during that era—unearthing Roman ruins and medieval plague pits. My destination site was near the Winchester Cathedral, a classic example of English Gothic architecture with one of the longest naves in all of Europe. It didn't matter that I had no background or experience in archaeology—the group just needed able bodies to do the digging and other grunt work. I had been saving up money since high school through babysitting and tutoring in my neighborhood and through my summer jobs at my mother's hospital, so I had just enough money for an airplane ticket and expenses for three months at the dig site.

My first ever ride on an airplane was a transatlantic flight with British Overseas Airways Corporation. Like Madonna, I had never been on an airplane in my life and was traveling alone! The flight attendant came down the aisle offering cocktails. I'd never had alcohol in my life either.

"Yes, I'll have vodka," I said.

"On the rocks?" she asked.

I had no idea what that meant, so I said no, and she gave it to me neat—but I didn't know what that meant either. I took a sip and thought I would die from poisoning.

My overseas adventure would be a trip of many other firsts and other moments of confusion. I was just figuring everything out as I went along.

I took a bus from Heathrow into London, and though I'd studied British currency—pounds, shillings, pence—I wasn't prepared for the colloquialisms and slang.

"It'll be seven bob," the bus driver said.

I had no idea what a "bob" was. I stretched out my hands full of coins.

"Can you just take out seven bob?"

He gave me a side glance and picked out seven shillings.

After the bus ride, I arrived at the site near the cathedral and found someone I assumed was one of the organizers. He led me to the upstairs loft of an abandoned warehouse that was being used as a boarding house for those on the dig. There was no electricity or nearby toilets, and the window panes were broken out. In the dim light I made out six beds.

The guide pointed to one of them and said, "That's your bed."

I couldn't see well enough to know who else was in the room. I changed clothes in the dark and went to bed. All night I listened to the draft rattling the shattered windows and heard the door to the sleeping area open and close as various people came and went.

The next morning, I got dressed and went to find breakfast. The group conducting the dig was providing room and board, but I quickly discovered that the lodging wasn't the only thing they'd skimped on. At every meal, breakfast, lunch and dinner, they fed us—of all things—stewed tomatoes. I hated tomatoes.

This adventure was not off to the best start.

The archaeological site itself was a large rectangular space that had been roped off and cut to a certain depth in the ground. I was part of a group of a dozen students, and we were assigned to a specific spot and given tools to remove and sift the dirt. I spent a couple of days digging and sifting dirt, another evening or two listening to the door to the sleeping area open and close, and another day of inedible food. After about three days I'd had enough. Perhaps this was how archaeologists were used to living during a dig, but I had not signed up for three months of eating stewed tomatoes and sleeping in a room where bats might fly in and out every night.

One morning I went to the bus terminal and asked how much it would cost to catch a bus out of Winchester—I wanted to be anywhere but there. Then I stopped by an outdoor supply store and bought a backpack and a tent and a few things I knew I might need thanks to all those summers at the beach or the mountains with my family. Once I was packed and ready, I announced to the archae-ologists that I was leaving.

The next bus took me to a train station, and the train took me to the white cliffs of Dover, and then a ferry took me across the English Channel to Dunkirk, France. On the Continent I slid out a map of Europe and made my way south through France and Italy. Once I started running out of money, I turned around and headed north through Austria, Switzerland, Germany, and Belgium before returning to England to catch my flight home. Along the way I camped in campsites just like Dad had taught us, though every now and then I stayed in a youth hostel so I could get a good shower.

The people I met and the beauty I encountered along the way were life changing! There was the time I wanted to get from Rome to Florence but couldn't find it on the map—because I had no idea that *Firenze* was Florence in Italian. Once I arrived in Firenze I went to visit *David*, the famous statue by Michelangelo, and sat before it, weeping at its magnificence. There was a messier moment when I was running in a skirt to catch a train bound to leave at any minute. A man running next to me dropped a soda bottle that shattered on the pavement and sent shards of glass into my bare leg. I kept running. Blood gushed from the open wound and people started pointing at me and calling out in either French or Italian. I couldn't quite understand what they were saying, but I realized soon enough I needed to do something about this gash on my shin. I found a local doctor a couple of blocks from the train station, and even though neither of us spoke the other's language, he cleaned me up, stitched and butterflied the wound, and sent me back to the station to catch the next train.

I hopped on and off lots of trains during that trip, sometimes even when they were moving. Those three months overseas helped stoke my sense of adventure; the trip coaxed me out of my shell and gave me more confidence in myself. I had lived such a structured, routine, protected life up until then, both at home and in college. In Europe I was truly on my own for the first time in my life. Figuring out train schedules, locating campgrounds, budgeting money so I could eat every day—all this taught me that I could get to where I needed to go and I could fend for myself in a variety of circumstances. Once, after visiting the *Mona Lisa*, I fell asleep outside on the steps of the Louvre, and no one bothered me. Looking back, I think I must have been crazy, but at the time I felt no fear.

The real fear was when I got back home. Toward the start of my trip, my parents had called the dig only to find out I had left early, and they had no other way of getting a hold of me. I sent postcards from the places to which I traveled, but it took six weeks for each of them to arrive—for the rest of my time in Europe, my parents never knew where I was. My dad was so sick with anxiety over my whereabouts and well-being that he couldn't even work. I didn't think about this grand adventure in terms of danger or putting myself at risk—the entire experience was exciting and empowering.

It would have been easy to have told myself I didn't have the experience in archeology nor the money to invest on being part of a dig in Winchester, just like it would have been easy for me to say I didn't have the time or the space to host a woman from Sierra Leone in my house in Nashville. I've learned ever since college to be open to new experiences, and to be willing to take chances.

Whether it's the financial market or it's life, you never know what sort of opportunities await you if you don't take chances.

*"Most people need love and acceptance
a lot more than they need advice."*
— BOB GOFF, *LOVE DOES: DISCOVER A SECRETLY
INCREDIBLE LIFE IN AN ORDINARY WORLD* (2012)

Chapter Ten

BUILD A SOLID FOUNDATION

TURNING OVER THE REINS

"Do you think you're doing what you need to be doing?"

The young man in his thirties sitting across from me in the boardroom looked surprised at my question. Ben worked for three older guys who were trying to build a start-up company and had just been promoted to vice president.

"Well, I'm trying to go out to hunt and kill something for my family," he said with a smile.

At the time, Ben was reading J. I. Packer and believed that God was not as interested in his vocation as He was interested in him being faithful to where he was at. *If God has something new for me*, Ben thought, *He will make it clear as sunrise.*

It was September 2012 when I met Ben. He was a successful businessman who knew one of the board members of Just Hope International. The board encouraged me that it was time to hire someone as JHI's president, and Ben's friend threw out his name. He agreed to meet with me on Labor Day weekend. This began a journey where I asked him the same question about passion that Dr. J. Howard Olds had asked me.

"What's your passion?" I asked Ben.

During our first meeting, I shared with him my journey of service and the *aha* moments I'd had. They reminded Ben of his own mission trips he took, ones such as going to Haiti with a church group and feeling like it was a little bit of a vacation, a little bit of an adventure, where you worked on a project but couldn't help wondering what the point of all the work was. He recalled digging ditches over a pathway so people could enter a church while local men stood there watching them work. Ben couldn't help wondering why they came all the way down there to do work these men could have been doing.

Before the meeting ended, I gave Ben two books that had become inspirational to my work in Just Hope International: *Toxic Charity: How Churches and Charities Hurt Those They Help (and How to Reverse It)* by Robert D. Lupton and *The Hole in Our Gospel* by Richard Stearns.

"Read these two books and tell me what you think," I told him.

Over the course of that fall, Ben and I discussed him taking over as president of Just Hope International. We attended a conference in Arizona where Robert Lupton was speaking so we had the opportunity to meet the author personally and have breakfast and dinner with him.

Bob put words, experience, and research to my intuition that somehow, people in need must be integrally involved in solving their own problems in order for the solutions to last. His book *Toxic Charity* was proof of my inklings in Peru, when I first began to sense the difference between "parity and charity," as he puts it. Bob opened my eyes to the problems with one-way giving. He outlined the sad arc that followed under the heading "Limit one-way giving to emergency situations":

- give once and you elicit appreciation
- give twice and you create anticipation
- give three times and you create expectation
- give four times and it becomes entitlement
- give five times and you establish dependency

These confirmed what I felt after realizing the food I gave to the children living in the trash dump in Nicaragua did not change a thing. So many of my prior trips involved handouts, and Bob's book both humbled me and lit a fire beneath me. In my heart, I knew it was more important to give a hand up rather than a handout, as I've noted. *Toxic Charity* and this list inside it let me know that Bob and I were on the same path. As we met, he shared personal examples with Ben and me on how he came to feel this way.

I knew I could use the gifts God had entrusted to me, not just to make people less poor for a day or a week, but for the rest of their lives! And because the people themselves would be working alongside the people of Just Hope, they would be responsible for their own success, and entitled not to handouts, but to the dignity that they received from having done it themselves. And having been taught and inspired, wouldn't the chances be great that they could then turn to a family member, a neighbor, perhaps even a stranger in a faraway land, and pass on the gift?

One of the many reasons for the need to hire someone to run Just Hope International was because of the practical issues I was having: I was also running a trading company. Sometimes in the middle of trading I might receive multiple phone calls from West Africa, for instance, asking me to send money so they could buy a truck or calls from somewhere else with another issue. I would then have to handle getting an international wire sent, all while continuing to run my trading company that provided the means to buy the truck in the first place.

As I talked to Ben about turning over the reins of the organization to him, I discovered that we both believed that business principles were the keys to truly alleviating poverty worldwide. Our philosophy was that capitalism is a tool that could be used for the good of many, not just the greed of a few.

Ben decided to give up his successful career and take over Just Hope at the end of 2012. I hired him on January 1, 2013.

We look back on this now and realize we were traveling down a similar path. We both were successful business people who gave that up to walk the road less traveled. And as the poet said, that has made all the difference.

LITTLE BY LITTLE

The reason we were able to hire Ben and for the growth of Just Hope International was because of the other road I was traveling down, the road of investing. It turned out the funds that I had been investing for my friends and former colleagues grew enough to allow me to underwrite all of Just Hope's overhead and operating costs.

One definition for the word *invest* is to "to use, give, or devote (time, talent, and so forth), as for a purpose or to achieve something."[4] This is exactly what I've done since 2007 when I left my career in the business world behind and followed God's calling. Instead of my time, effort, and energy being centered around producing financial results, however, they were all for the purpose of helping to grow Just Hope International. We were a 501(c)(3) charity that functioned off independent donations. I just needed to figure out how to pay my monthly living expenses. That's where the other definition of *invest* comes in.

4 https://www.dictionary.com/browse/invest?s=t

I started with spending $10,000 to learn how to trade. Then I invested my savings and IRA into a trading account. Sure enough, the money I started to make off these investments paid for my bills.

From the very beginning, I made a promise to everyone I spoke to that 100 percent of their donation to Just Hope International would go to the projects I was working on. Never a penny has gone toward any type of administrative expense. I've paid that out of my own pocket. Not that administrative expenses are bad things; those are necessary. It was just my personal commitment.

I look back and see all the steps God allowed me to take to provide for myself and JHI. The lunch with someone who soon convinced me to start investing his money for him. The JHI trips I took in 2008 where I would work during the day and then trade late at night. The trusted friend whom I asked to come work with me. Another friend who also invested with us. The pot of money just kept growing and growing and we were becoming very successful. Then others began to hear of our success. I was continually being approached by people to invest some of their money. I approached my two friends and asked if they would have a problem with me opening up a trading company where I could handle other peoples' money.

The truth has always been that I never began to start trading just to make money, and I never built an investment company just to produce profits. I responded to what my friends wanted me to do for them. It was little by little by little, and then all of a sudden, I was investing over $200 million.

When I opened Hope Investments in 2011, the initial investment was $1.3 million. My goal was to increase that to $5 million by the year's end. At the end of December 2011, the investment pool was at $42 million. This meant I had to continue to hire people as the fund grew. At one time, I had six employees. These people weren't just employees, they were all my friends. A few of them I had known for twenty years.

When I first established Just Hope International, I assumed it would be a project that would live and die with me. I never imagined it could blossom into something much bigger. Making a lot of money and putting it all in my pocket were never goals of mine.

Yet I knew that my skill set could be used to further God's work in the world. I consider my success in trading to be a God-given gift, and I knew I needed to continue to walk in faith by allowing Just Hope International to expand. By the end of 2011, with the financial blessings of Hope Investments, I realized God had greater plans for JHI that went well beyond my original vision.

This was why I established the Just Hope Foundation in 2012 and invested 50 percent of all the income made by Hope Investments into the foundation. This income would fully fund JHI's operational overhead. As a result, 100 percent of donor contributions could be routed directly to program expenses.

"Slow and steady wins the race."

—FROM *AESOP'S FABLES:*

A NEW TRANSLATION (1912)

Chapter Eleven

REMAIN PATIENT

LIFE IS SWIRLING ALONG

"The Tortoise and the Hare" might be the most well known story of *Aesop's Fables*. After an arrogant hare mocks the slow-moving tortoise, the latter challenges the hare to a race. After leaping to a huge lead and knowing he is going to win, the hare takes a nap, only to awaken and realize he's lost the race.

When it comes to both my trading and to impacting lives in impoverished countries, my approach has always been representative of the tortoise. But that's not how I was when Ben started work at Just Hope International; there was no slow and steady pace I had in store for him. On his first day I showed him where he would be working and where I traded and then gave him some materials to look over.

"By the way," I added before leaving him. "In three weeks we are going to Sierra Leone. You will get to meet the people we're working with."

Ben definitely hit the ground running!

In Africa, it is said that "water is life." So you can imagine our excitement when we made another critical trip to our new project site in Sierra Leone to drill two boreholes (water wells) on our property. We were reminded to be thankful that we live in a country where access to clean water was not something we had to think about.

After a whole year of preparing and waiting, we traveled eight thousand miles in a couple of days to be present for the drilling. People and groups from several states had contributed financially for this effort. But when we arrived, the work was delayed. It frustrated me because we had a tight schedule to keep.

Sometimes I even had to be reminded of the slow and deliberate tortoise. I wrote about this in my journal:

> *What seems to be important in my daily life is my schedule. What am I supposed to accomplish today? When? With whom? The drilling for the boreholes was supposed to begin on Tuesday. That did not happen. Neither did the drilling begin on Wednesday, Thursday, or Friday. It was very frustrating. We had a schedule to maintain! What I realized during those days when the drilling was*

not happening, was that life was swirling
along all around me.

Amid the delay, Ben and I were in Bauya, standing next to our truck on a dirt road, when a local woman appeared carrying her son. His name was Lansana and both of his legs were severely infected and losing tissue; thus, he was unable to walk. Since Lansana couldn't walk, his mother carried him eight miles hoping that one of us could help him. Her hopes were dashed, however, when none of us knew what to do for him. Our attention shifted from wondering "why" the equipment had failed to "what" to do in this situation. It was one thing to give distant thought to the plight of people suffering in the world. It was another to be face-to-face with it and feel the weight of their circumstances.

The child's face told us everything we needed to know; he was in a lot of pain. It was the afternoon and Ben and I were about to return to where we were staying. We told the mother we couldn't do anything at the moment, so we drove Lansana and her back to their community. We asked about what could be done and then returned to them the next day.

Lansana did not have access to medical care for two reasons: Medical care was not available where he lived, and the family had no money to travel to where it existed or to pay for the services once there.

Maybe this is why we're here.

After a mental shift away from what we were there to do and toward the people God had put in front of us, we marshaled our resources and found a hospital where we knew we could take the child the next day. We returned to his community the next day, picked up the child and his mother, and transported them to a clinic where his infections were treated and his legs were saved. We paid for the service and left the hospital to return to our work in Bauya. We stayed in touch with Lansana and learned that the little boy's wounds healed with time. He returned to typical childhood behavior, with a big smile on his face.

It was wonderful to be able to help people, but the experience also illustrated the problem I had been trying to fix. The solution to Lansana's problem was completely dependent upon us. This experience once again confirmed for us that we wanted to be in the business of getting ahead of the problem, of fixing the broken part of the system that prevented people from having their own income and their own ability to take care of their families, so that when an infection came along, it was cured quickly and without a child's pain, without a mother's deep worry, and without a family having to choose between feeding a son or saving his legs.

The trip also reinforced that sometimes we couldn't be so focused and narrow-minded to miss what was happening in other places. I realized on this trip that on the days when the drilling was not happening, the life around me continued to be lived. There was the woman who walked eight miles to carry her sick child to us hoping we could help him; the small village we could reach only by foot, where we were greeted by friendly people and saw poor children running around without clothing; the impromptu soccer match that broke out; meeting an eighty-year-old man on the road who spent about an hour telling us about the life he had lived in that area; and even the little girl who had never seen a white person who crossed my path in the jungle and screamed at the top of her lungs.

Each of these events left a trace on my soul and made me realize that, had I been rushing and fixated on the drilling machine, I would have missed all these experiences I had each of those days.

THE STRATEGY OF PATIENCE

"Each day my mother demonstrated great patience and the ability and eagerness to work very hard without complaint."[5]

John Wooden said that, and if anybody understands excellence, it's this man. He is considered the greatest NCAA basketball head coach of all time after leading the UCLA Bruins to ten NCAA men's basketball championships. This included winning seven championships in a row from 1967 to 1973.

"The Wizard of Westwood" knew the value of patience in sports and in life. In his celebrated autobiography, *They Call Me Coach,* Wooden shared his views on this:

5 Wooden, John. *Wooden: A Lifetime of Observations and Reflections On and Off the Court.* New York: McGraw-Hill Professional Publishing, 1997.

*In game play it was always my philos-
ophy that patience would win out. By that, I
meant patience to follow our game plan. If we
believed in it, we would wear the opposition
down and would eventually get to them. If
we broke away from our style, however, and
played their style, we would be in trouble.
And if we let our emotions, rather than our
reason, command the game we would not
function effectively.*[6]

Emotions are a dangerous thing when it comes
to investing. Many investors that I have met over
all these years allow two strong emotions to take
over: greed or fear. They make decisions to take a
risk on making a lot of money out of greed, or they
make decisions out of fear of what is going on in the
market. I tell people to get that out of their heads.
If you are trading through emotion, then you will
likely be making mistakes that you wouldn't make
if you took the emotion out of it. Fortunately for me,

6 Wooden, John. *The Wizard of Westwood: Coach John
   Wooden and His UCLA Bruins.* Boston: Houghton and
   Mifflin, 1973.

it comes natural to just look at this as numbers. I want the numbers to increase and know what to do to make that happen without taking a lot of risk.

Even as Hope Investments grew from $5 million to $42 million in a year, I never looked at this as a large amount of money. It was never money to me; it was only numbers and figures. I never chase money in the market. Investing comes so naturally to me that I just do it without much thought. I just look at the market and know what to do. I invest wisely and safely; it may be safe at the time I invest, but with a strong market move, it becomes unsafe, and I have a process to return to safety. It may take a while, but I try my best not to lose money.

When I began trading, I took my time to learn how to do it. I enrolled in courses on trading, traveled to different cities on the weekends to attend seminars on trading, read a lot of books, and learned from all my failures in my trading. I started as a fundamental trader, studying a company's balance sheet, income statement, and annual report. As a CPA, this is all that made sense to me. But when some of the companies I researched and selected to invest in lost a lot of money due to circumstances that had nothing to do with their financial state-ments, I knew I had a choice to make. Either quit investing for myself or learn from my mistakes. I decided the best was to learn from my mistakes and I became a technical trader, which I still am today. And I moved from stocks to trading options.

A technical trader uses historical patterns to predict what might happen in the future, and from what I see, I always attempt to trade very cautiously. I don't want to take a lot of risk. Sometimes the market turns against you and you have to persevere. It may take time but, more times than not, you can work your way out of a severe market turn.

I refer to the tortoise and hare story a lot when it comes to how I operate. My determination, my steadfastness, and my ability to make money in the market puts me in the tortoise category. As I always tell everybody, I might be the tortoise, but I always get to the finish line.

"We ourselves feel that what we are doing is just a drop in the ocean. But if the drop was not in the ocean, I think the ocean would be less because of the missing drop."
—MOTHER TERESA, *MOTHER TERESA'S REACHING OUT IN LOVE* (2002)

Chapter Twelve

DO IT WITH PURPOSE

THE WHAT

Some people seem born with purpose. Especially those who might not have ever been born in the first place.

In September 1958, a young pregnant wife ended up in the hospital for what was mistaken to be an appendicitis attack. After treating her, the doctors suggested that she abort her child since it would surely be born with some kind of disability.

"But the courageous young wife decided not to terminate the pregnancy and the child was born. The woman was my mother, I was the child.[7]"

The man telling this story is Andrea Bocelli, one of the world's most famous singers with more than thirty albums selling more than ninety million records. Bocelli was born partially blind, only to lose the rest of his vision in a soccer accident when he was twelve years old. This didn't stop him from finding a passion and a purpose in his life.

7   John Hooper, "Tenor's story acclaimed by anti-abortion campaigners," *The Guardian*, 10 June 2010, https://www. theguardian.com/world/2010/jun/10/andrea-bocelli-abortion-italy (accessed 19 February 2021).

In July 2011, Bocelli started a foundation named after him in order to give back to others after having experienced a life where many have been very generous to him.

"When I was a boy, I asked for help too," he says on the Andrea Bocelli Foundation website. "I knew the condition of being in need too, I looked for support, for assistance from my close friends and family. After that, I had the chance, or better the joy, to be able to give back: a growing desire to help, becoming a responsibility, a binding priority, and an ethical duty." He continues, "Over the years, I tried to make myself useful in the best ways I could, but I had the feeling that it was not enough."[8]

The Andrea Bocelli Foundation was established with definitive purpose in mind. As Bocelli explains, "I strongly believe that love does justice. And it is for this simple reason that we are all responsible for building a better world. Since love energizes faith, the opposite must also be true. The amazing lives we have been gifted offer us the privilege, opportunity,

8 "Letter from the Founder," Andrea Bocelli Foundation, https://www.andreabocellifoundation.org/who-we-are/letter-from-the-founder/ (accessed 21 March 2021).

and responsibility to give the less fortunate a better future and opportunities."[9]

Can't you see why I just love this man?

Andrea Bocelli found his purpose early on in his life despite the hardships he experienced. His foundation has adopted that purpose in order to help others. Once you know and define your purpose, the next steps are to find creative ways to put that into action.

Just Hope's mission is not just to make an impact but to make an impact that lasts. This means engaging in projects that will succeed long term once we are no longer around. One such project began in 2013 and involves pineapples. *A lot* of pineapples.

As we looked at Sierra Leone and the best ways to help, we examined the key priorities among those living there. These are education, agriculture, and well-being. The best chance to achieve these goals is

9 "Mission and Vision," Andrea Bocelli Foundation. https://www.andreabocellifoundation.org/who-we-are/mission-and-vision/ (accessed 21 March 2021).

to earn enough income to buy food and get medical supplies. Just Hope decided to pilot an economic development program based around a five-acre pineapple farm in Bauya, Sierra Leone, that Just Hope created.

So why pineapples?

Just Hope sees pineapple farming as an *income opportunity*. We leverage local farming skills, assist with start-up needs, and connect farmers to a commercial pineapple buyer, giving access to good-paying, agriculture-based jobs that allow locals to provide for their families and rebuild their communities. Local growers sell their harvest in a simple, straightforward way to a local pineapple buyer we've identified, one who has long-term plans and the infrastructure to operate in Sierra Leone.

In addition to producing pineapple fruits that can be sold to the buyer, the pineapple plant also produces seedlings commonly called "suckers." A sucker is the starter for a new plant. One pineapple plant makes several suckers, so one acre of a pine-apple crop can become a three-acre crop in just a couple of crop cycles. Suckers can be used to plant a new crop, increase the following year's crop, or be sold and shared with other families.

In the fall of 2013, we worked with several dozen workers in Bauya to complete planting five acres of pineapple plants that produced ninety thousand plants in total. The plan was for these plants to fruit in about eighteen months and also to provide two suckers per plant, which could be removed and used to start new plants. But we had other purposes in mind with the pineapples. We wanted to provide an agricultural and technical training location for people and to present a new farming idea for locals to consider, all while facilitating a way for people to start farms independent of Just Hope.

There are multiple purposes for these pineapple farms. At the family level, the income from selling pineapples is good money for rural families. Considering their priorities, this money can be used to pay for education, food, and medical care needed for good health and nourishment. From a big picture and long-term point of view, learning to grow pineapples is agricultural knowledge that cannot be taken away.

One of the most rewarding parts of our initial efforts was when we identified and offered an opportunity to three groups of locals. Joseph, Abu, and Dauda become our first farming entre- preneurs, with each committing to farm an acre of pineapples. This matched the purpose of Just Hope. We were not giving these men a handout, since those erode personal dignity and may damage local industry and economies. Handouts often lead to dependency. Instead, we know that people are remarkable—and with the right training and opportunity, people can do remark- able things. Each person has God-given talents, abilities, interests, and motivations that, when connected with the necessary training, mentor- ship, and resources, have the power to transform families and communities. The greatest chance for lasting change in people's lives comes from empowering them to provide for themselves.

An interesting story occurred while I was at the pineapple plantation one day working with a group of local men. They were chopping limbs off the palm trees so the ground was covered with palm leaves. One man began shouting, taking his long, curved blade and striking the ground with it. He chopped the head off an eight-foot-long venomous green mamba. They also killed four small cobras that were about eighteen inches long. I got out of the field when this happened. They took rocks, placed them in a small circle, made a fire in the center and cooked the snakes and also a few rats and snails. They invited me to dinner that night, but I declined.

Twenty workers are employed in the planting of the suckers. They plant approximately 3,500 suckers per day on land that they previously prepared by removing brush and stumps. Prime planting season is early in the year before the rainy season begins in May and workers can cease manual irrigation of the acres of pineapple suckers in the ground.

Even the pineapple has a purpose. As a member of the bromeliad family, the pineapple plant is naturally drought resistant, making it ideal for the climate in this area where many weeks can pass without rain during the dry season. Its strength comes from its resilience.

THE WHY

In many ways, the principles that guide Just Hope resemble the ones that I have had in my investing life. I have never formally listed them out and made them part of some sort of plan and purpose with my trading, but as I reflect on both, I realize they match up well together.

The first guiding principle of Just Hope is *income opportunity*. Our goal is to economically empower women and men to transform their family and community for generations. As individuals and families work to obtain financial independence, they reclaim their dignity, envision new possibilities, and experience the power of hope.

Isn't this what everybody wants as they begin to start investing? They want to strengthen their family and their future. This started with me when I left my employer and began to start trading using my 401K, all with the purpose to make enough money to pay my bills. That money would empower my greater purpose with the work we did in Just Hope.

The next guiding principle is to have *local leadership*. This builds trust through accountability in the field. All Just Hope projects are supervised by trustworthy, qualified managers who are invested in the community and are locals themselves.

My trading process was developed from learning the hard way, having failures and learning from that, and then finally having success. Since I know this is a God-given talent, I share the things I've learned with whomever asks me about it. It's a gift I love to share. Those who knew me and trusted me asked me to invest for them, so that's where my trading began. I wasn't just good at what I did, I was also invested in the people I was trading for.

The third principle for Just Hope is *ownership matters*. This means having smart business processes, from assessment through exit. At the core of the Just Hope project model are opportunities that are simple, repeatable, and viable given the local circumstances. All projects follow an established process that starts with an assessment, moves through project execution, and concludes with an exit strategy. Our partners have ownership of projects from the start, so they require no long-term outside resources.

Successful businesses are disciplined in following simple and repeatable processes that achieve their goals. My trading has been that way, especially when I stopped trading stocks. It got me out of the guessing game of wondering whether it was going up or down. When I moved over to options and then moved over to the indexes, I could play more safely. As I built my strategy, it became a very simple strategy.

You need to have principles in place to fulfill your purpose. The question is, what is your purpose?

A quote by writer and theologian Frederick Buechner sums up my life: "The place God calls you to is the place where your deep gladness and the world's deep hunger meet."[10]

In 2016, I was reminded of my purpose in life when I learned I would be receiving the

10 Frederick Buechner, "Vocation," *Wishful Thinking: A Theological ABC* (Glasgow: William Collins, Sons), 1973.

Distinguished Alumni Award from my alma mater, the University of North Carolina. It was such an honor for my career and my humanitarian work to be recognized like this. I'm not a person who spends much time or effort looking back in life, but I was encouraged to review my past in preparation to share my appreciation to those at the event. I decided to contemplate on the what and the why of my life's calling.

The *what* was easy to describe. How in 2007 I left my career behind and founded a nonprofit called Just Hope. I spoke about our efforts and the principles behind it. But the *why*—that involves the purpose behind all these efforts.

"The why is the most important part," I said in my speech. "And the why is about one word: *compassion*. God manifests Himself in the compassion that we show one another. I believe each of us has a special gift, a special talent. And I believe our purpose in life is to use that talent to make a difference in the world. And that can be in our home, locally, nationally, or internationally. And I believe through our actions, we bring the kingdom of God to where we are, right here, right now."

In a video that focused on my life and my calling, several people shared their thoughts about me on film. One person to contribute was Tom Sosnoff, a former trader who cofounded the online financial network tastytrade. He had seen not just the trading side of my life but also knew the reasons *why* I traded.

"You're talking about a very rare person," Tom said. "This is not somebody that had a liquidation event like an IPO or something for a hundred million or billion dollars or ten billion dollars. This is somebody who is incredibly self-made at a certain point in life when it's very difficult to reach that level of achievement. Then to turn around and make the contributions she's made for goodwill? Pretty amazing."

These were gracious words and I can honestly say I'm simply following God's calling in my life—a purpose that began to unfold inside of me when Dr. J. Howard Olds asked me about my passion years ago.

THE LAMB OF WALL STREET

Andrea Bocelli found his purpose and passion early on in his life, and he has shared that amazing gift with the rest of the world. With efforts like starting his foundation, he has put that purpose into action.

"I am sure you will then agree with my modest thought that sparked the project of the foundation and that has become its mission," Bocelli said. "Our faith in love and justice calls upon us to build a better world than the one we found; it calls upon us to give back to the community all the good things that we have received, so that the less fortunate or the most vulnerable members of our society will have a chance to achieve a life full of opportunities and beauty, so that those who take up the challenge will find the energy and real possibilities to thrive in their lives."[11]

Those who take up the challenge.

I feel like I first took up the challenge when I took a deep look at my faith and decided to help build a better world. I found a deeper and richer

11 "Letter from the Founder," Andrea Bocelli Foundation. https://www.andreabocellifoundation.org/who-we-are/ mission-and-vision/ (accessed 21 March 2021).

purpose in my life, a purpose, as Bocelli said, "to give back to the community all the good things that we have received."

Ben, the man who is now president of Just Hope, perhaps summed up purpose the best with a simple but profound illustration. One day in the office, he shared his thoughts with me by quoting a popular saying.

"Karen, you know—it's just all about the dash."

For a moment I didn't understand what he was saying. "What dash?"

"The dash on our tombstones," Ben said. "There is the date we were born and the date we died, and in between there is a dash."

So that's the question for all of us. What are we doing with our dash?

*"Hoping for the best, prepared for the worst,
and unsurprised by anything in between."*
—MAYA ANGELOU,
I KNOW WHY THE CAGED BIRD SINGS (1969)

Chapter Thirteen

EXPECT THE UNEXPECTED

THE FRUITS OF OUR LABORS

One day when I was a little girl, my brother and I were out riding our bicycles. I committed what was to Larry an egregious error—I rode my bike onto the neighborhood's "boys only" bike path. Girls were not allowed on that path. In response, my brother rammed his bicycle into mine. I wiped out so badly that most of my front teeth got knocked out.

The whole family made the trip to the dentist. Mom held me screaming and bloody in the passenger seat while Larry was relegated to the back. Dad drove a few blocks and then pulled the car over to beat my brother with a rolled-up copy of *The Charlotte Observer*. Mom calmed him down, and we went another few blocks before Dad pulled over and took the paper to Larry's hide all over again. With that rhythm, it took a while to get to the dentist office.

My brother and I became dear friends in adulthood. He liked to point out I had a speech impediment as a kid and couldn't form my words very well. After he knocked out my front teeth and the dentist put me back together again, that speech problem somehow cleared itself up. I guess unexpected blows can sometimes help a girl find her voice.

Life resembles that story. You never know what tomorrow might bring, what door might open, and what person might walk through.

I heard my steps rustling over the trail as I walked through the forest. I had been working in the pine-apple field in Sierra Leone, and I was walking down a long, narrow path to take me to another village. The dense jungle stood on each side of me. Halfway down the path, I spotted a little local girl heading my way carrying a big pail of water from the local river. She obviously was taking it home. When she saw me, she stopped and screamed, dropping the bucket and turning to run in the other direction.

Her screams followed her as she ran away from me.

It took me fifteen minutes to reach the village and step off that jungle path. When I got to the other end, local men stood there waiting for me.

The terrified little girl hid behind one of the men with her arms wrapped around his leg. One of the villagers who spoke English explained to me what was happening.

"She is saying 'white devil, white devil,' " he told me.

The petrified child had never seen a white person, so she thought I was the devil. One of the men, amused by the girl's reaction, picked her up and tried to shove her toward me. I told him to stop that and leave the little girl alone. The men tried to reassure the girl, telling her I was not Satan.

So many fears we carry with us are unfounded and unnecessary. Even when it seems like the very worst thing might happen, the Bible instructs us time and time again to not be anxious. In Isaiah 41:10 it reads, "So do not fear, for I am with you; do not be dismayed, for I am your God. I will strengthen you and help you; I will uphold you with my righteous right hand" (NIV). The great Psalm 27:1 says (also in the NIV), "The Lord is my light and my salvation—whom shall I fear? The Lord is the stronghold of my life—of whom shall I be afraid?"

This light and hope became even more necessary when in 2014 we were faced with legitimate fears about an epidemic threatening the population. Just as Just Hope's pineapple farm was literally taking root, our entire operation was suddenly hampered by the outbreak of the deadly Ebola virus. The disastrous epidemic threatened the population, including Just Hope workers and their families, and led to unexpected consequences for our farm projects.

The World Health Organization (WHO) first reported in March 2014 about a major Ebola outbreak happening in the West African country of Guinea. Soon Sierra Leone and Liberia documented cases themselves. On August 8, WHO declared the situation a Public Health Emergency of International Concern, and a month later they issued a statement about the danger of this virus. "The Ebola epidemic ravaging parts of West Africa is the most severe acute public health emergency seen in modern times. Never before in recorded history has a biosafety level four pathogen infected so many people so quickly, over such a broad geographical area, for so long."[12] Ebola eventually spread to seven additional countries, including the United States and the United Kingdom.

Suddenly all of our work on the pineapple farm came into question. Fear of the unknown filled all of us.

In our line of work, the phrase *subject to change* is common in our vocabulary. Solid, well-formed plans are without question a necessary component of our success. And yet the plans, and we who implement them, must remain flexible because circumstances change. Sometimes on a dime. We certainly experienced an extreme dose of this in Sierra Leone.

Starting in the summer of 2014, Ebola swept through Sierra Leone, causing thousands of deaths, travel bans, border closings, quarantines, school closings, and an annihilation of the fragile economy that existed. The company that offered to buy our harvest lost nearly every one of their expatriate

12 "Experimental therapies: growing interest in the use of whole blood or plasma from recovered Ebola patients (convalescent therapies)," World Health Organization, 26 September 2014. https://www.who.int/mediacentre/news/ebola/26-september-2014/en/ (accessed 21 March 2021).

managers and workers, who headed home when the seriousness of the situation became clear.

We held steady, praying that Ebola would be contained and eliminated, for the sake of all the people of Sierra Leone mainly, but also so our workers in Bauya would still have an economic opportunity at harvest time. Our "boots on the ground," Sullay and Joseph, faithfully managed the project, and ushered through the rainy season and into the dry season a most beautiful crop of pine-apple plants.

In mid-January 2015, about six months away from anticipated harvest time, and as the Ebola epidemic started to show signs of containment, we encountered another turn in the road: pineapples. Gorgeous pineapples, sitting up proud and colorful on strong stalks, but arriving entirely too early. Since pineapple plants have stout, sawlike leaves that are as sharp as razors, a field of mature plants growing in tight rows alongside one another was impenetrable without special pants and other gear. We found ourselves without this special gear since we didn't expect to need the gear until that summer, and due to the fact that the borders between Bauya and Freetown, where the gear could be bought, were closed.

When the borders finally reopened weeks later, Sullay made a trip into Freetown to purchase the pants, safety glasses, boots, and gloves so that he could investigate how many pineapples we had. Our pineapple buyer was not up and running again but was looking hopefully at the month of May. If it was just a few pineapples, and the majority of the crop appeared to be on schedule for a summer harvest, it was possible that we could get back on track with our original plan. If the entire crop was fruiting, then we would have a challenge indeed.

There was a period of huge relief when we received word from the processing plant that they expected to be operational whenever our harvest arrived. Representatives from the plant visited our pineapple farm and trained Sullay, Joseph, and the crew how to "force" the pineapples to fruit using calcium carbide. The purpose of forcing them was to maximize the number that fruited all at once, which created efficiencies in harvesting and trans-porting. The processing plant ended up closing, however, forcing us to execute our backup plan to sell the fruit on the local fresh market. Graciously, the plant loaned us their trucks and drivers to pick up the harvest and deliver it to the Luma, the nearest market to Bauya.

Our crew was able to harvest and deliver three loads of pineapples, amounting to about eight thousand pineapples total. They did a great job in spite of the wet weather. Much like our outdoor markets and activities there, heavy rains drastically reduced the number of people in attendance, increasing the number of days it took to sell a load. Sullay and our team continued to learn about pineapples, including harvesting, loading, shelf life in a hot truck, sales, and "what stage of ripe" the customer base was looking for. We had adjusted our selection process for harvest, and it seemed to be paying off.

Sullay and Joe found another market, where people were sending trucks to the site to buy fruit in bulk, and we ended up selling many pineapples through that market. The selling price was lower than the more urban market; however, the net profit was almost the same if not slightly higher, as we did not have the expenses associated with a three-day selling trip, such as fuel, food, and overnight costs.

We were able to hire back some of the women who served as temporary workers earlier in the season and who had assisted with planting and watering. They now assisted in the harvest and transported the pineapples to the vehicle collection point. This provided them with valuable additional income for that time of year, known as "the hungry months" because food stores were getting low and new crops were not yet producing.

When Ben and I arrived in Bauya in September 2015, we inspected the farm and made the difficult decision to cease harvesting due to fruit spoilage. Our harvest window came and went very quickly for several reasons: all plants had been forced to ripen at the same time in preparation for a juicing harvest that was thwarted by the shutdown of the juicing processor; heavy rains made for a slow fresh-market sellout; and government law did not allow Sunday markets. Some local will-call markets absorbed many of the fruits, as did some of the people in the village. A small number of pineapples continued to ripen, but the quantity did not justify the cost of fuel or transportation to market. Sullay reported many were being given to school children, and some were being taken as gifts to people in the new community health office that had opened in Bauya in the last month.

After the many struggles we faced with Ebola and the often-limited access to information of plant status, it was heartening that many of our employees still wanted to be pineapple farmers. They had learned so much about the process of planting, maintaining, forcing, and sales that many were now clearing land for their own pineapple farms. We provided them with the suckers from our crop to help them get started. It was a bittersweet feeling to leave the community in the hands of the locals.

Our original plan of a single harvest and sale to a juice processor wasn't able to happen, but we adjusted and ended up selling the fruit in local fresh markets. The workers carefully harvested the number of pineapples we expected to be able to sell as they reached the correct stage of ripeness. Shifting gears in the name of success was part of this story, and we knew that flexibility and contingency planning were critical to success in our work, as it was with life in general. The resilience among the people of Sierra Leone with whom we worked was a blessing throughout this process, and we were grateful to God for the experience of working with people who were so full of hope, so strong in their resolve, and so motivated to succeed.

Seeing this venture through—from planting the suckers to managing a profitable harvest—was a powerful experience for the workers in Sierra Leone. Seeing the "fruit of their labor" going to market demonstrated that markets for large quantities exist and were accessible, opening their eyes to significant opportunities for their future.

THE WEIGHT OF THE WORLD

When the unexpected happens, you have to adjust and make the most out of the situation. The Ebola outbreak in 2014 couldn't have been helped, but we managed as best we could. The same was true for 2020 when a new and more deadly virus shut down the world.

Expect the unexpected and make the most out of the situation, whether it's in your job or life or in the world of trading.

At the end of February 2020, the market started falling but I never expected it to fall as dramatically as it did. On February 20, the S&P 500 was at approximately 3382. By March 23, it was at 2192. That is an extraordinary fall and it was attributed to COVID-19. Then the market went into a "backwardation" mode. In a normal market, generally the prices for options are higher at longer maturities and lower as you get closer to the current expiration date. Backwardation is just the opposite of that, and it creates some very challenging times. I must say that I've learned a great deal about trading in this market that I had never done before. It took ingenuity and just taking some chances to have traveled through this market. I managed, but I certainly hope I never have to deal with this again. But if I do, I'll be ready for it.

So how can you pivot and make the most out of a bad situation? We found a way during the Ebola epidemic and the pineapple dilemma. New cases and deaths were rising quickly, and the World

Health Organization and Centers for Disease Control (CDC) estimated that with no intervention, cases could reach well over one million by the spring of 2015. We knew we weren't a relief organization, but we were in a position to help and knew we must.

As with all projects, we started with an assessment. We consulted organizations on the ground, including the CDC's Sierra Leone Response Team. The largest need was patient transport to move infected people out of their homes to prevent the spread of Ebola. We then began planning and formed a partnership with World Hope International, which had medical teams already in place. World Hope committed to oversee the ambulance project, including hiring drivers and training them on safe patient interaction. With that partnership in place, we executed a plan to purchase and deliver five Toyota Land Cruisers to Sierra Leone.

These vehicles were put in service the first week of January 2015, with World Hope offices in Makeni (the capital city of the Bombali district) serving as the home base. When the ambulances arrived, the rate of new cases was slowing, and the need for the ambulances shifted from transporting sick patients to transporting survivors, those who tested negative, and orphans who had been quarantined for three weeks in treatment centers. Most people in Sierra Leone do not have access to personal transportation, and the country has no functioning ambulance service. Without a way home, many would not be able to leave the treatment center or return home to their families, who likely didn't know if they were dead or alive.

In their four-month deployment, the five ambulances traveled more than 33,000 kilometers (about 20,500 miles) and transported approximately 750 people. Six locals were hired full-time to drive the ambulances, earning exceptional driving and medical experience. One of the greatest accomplishments, however, was unexpected.

Carrie Jo, RN, program manager for World Hope International, helped operate the ambulance program in Sierra Leone's Bombali district. She described the environment before the ambulances arrived as chaotic, with no way to get sick people into treatment centers, and no way to get well people home.

When they arrived, the ambulances were immediately put to use returning well patients to their homes, which achieved two important benefits. The first was freeing up room and resources in treatment centers. The second was reuniting people with their families. An unexpected and beautiful side effect of this second benefit was that the ambulance service communicated to villages that Ebola was survivable, and that people who returned were immune, not contagious, and safe to welcome back home. Drivers were trained in sensitizing communities to these facts, and survivors returning home by ambulance were no longer shunned or rejected by their communities. This is important to note because communities that accept returning survivors are likely to recover from an epidemic more quickly due to their increased ability to pick up the pieces of their former lives. Without that recovery, economic empowerment would be further out of reach in the wake of this tumultuous epidemic.

The six locals hired as drivers received valuable driving and healthcare experience and training. These drivers—Mohamed (an Ebola survivor himself), Bakar K., Samuel, Rashid, Bakar J., and Nathaniel—were the heart of this program. Indeed, at a survivor conference of about three hundred, the drivers were the "heroes" and the ones the attendees all wanted to see, hug, and thank. While the effort with the ambulances was a deviation toward the area of relief and away from empowerment, Just Hope stayed true to our process of assessing, planning, executing by partnering with experts, and now, exiting.

Like anyone else, the people we serve face crises from time to time: the unexpected death of a family member, a flood, a crop failure. The difference is that their crises or "shocks" come while they are already in survival mode. And there are no safety nets, no government programs, to fall back on. For many people, the desire to pull themselves up is there, but without access to resources of any kind, there is no hope of making this desire a reality. Hopelessness adds to the suffering, and fear keeps them weighed down.

I love this quote from Max Lucado's book *Fearless:*

> *Fear never wrote a symphony or poem, negotiated a peace treaty or cured a disease. Fear never pulled a family out of poverty or a country out of bigotry. Fear never saved a marriage or a business. Courage did that. Faith did that. People who refused to consult or cower to their timidities did that. But fear itself? Fear herds us into prison and slams the doors.*[13]

So how do those of us confronting these issues daily deal with the apparent hopelessness and fears? Who else but *from the people we serve*. One key way is celebrating the little things along the way, no matter what the circumstances are. Some might call this joy. A prerequisite is definitely gratitude.

When the objects of your daily attention are suffering and hopelessness in the world, the need to celebrate the little things intensifies all the more.

13 Lucado, Max. *Fearless: Imagine Your Life Without Fear.* Nashville: Thomas Nelson Inc, 2009.

As a nonprofit focused on empowering people, we recognize the people we serve are remarkable in many ways. These individuals, families, and communities face living conditions and threats to their well-being every day that the average American cannot fathom, much less survive themselves.

We are making an effort to celebrate the little victories occurring among the people we serve: a robust harvest, a child finally able to attend school, a farmer expressing interest in improved techniques. We are celebrating the little things we see in one another as a support team here in the United States too. In this, we find ourselves having more similarities than differences with people around the world. Everywhere, celebrating little things is like focusing on just the next step, even when a marathon looms ahead.

What weighs you down? As a friend once asked, "What is weighing down that sled you are dragging behind you?" Take note from people who have nothing according to the world—celebrate the little things along the way. Don't forget the joy and gratitude to get you started. I'm finding it to be a very rich experience.

"Those who prosper in life know that endurance is the key to success."

—Neil T. Anderson,

The Daily Discipler (2005)

Chapter Fourteen

ENDURE AND PERSEVERE

GRACE AND COURAGE

We all have stories. So many of the best ones tell tales of struggling to survive and overcoming the odds. People love to hear about persevering in the midst of life's hardships because every single one of us has our own trials and battles. It's easy to wallow in our own troubles until we walk alongside others and realize all of us struggle.

Life isn't about comparing our wounds and scars and seeing who has the bigger ones. Life is about walking alongside others and listening to them. Empathizing with them. Learning from them. And most of all, loving them.

One such individual we were able to walk alongside was Saffie. She and her husband, Foday, became invaluable partners to Just Hope in Lunsar, Sierra Leone, graciously inviting us into their community and facilitating our work there to train and equip pastors and their families. Saffie was a child when the Sierra Leone civil war erupted, and a young mother before it was over ten years later. You could never believe the sort of things she had been through until she shared it herself.

One of her most vivid memories of the war was when rebels ambushed her village. She was holding her eight-month-old daughter in her arms, and the sudden surprise of the soldiers made her drop her baby. While her girl wasn't harmed, many others were brutally killed. Saffie witnessed a man, with both his arms cut off by rebels, fall and die in front of her, and saw a young boy kidnapped right before her eyes.

As a result of the war, countless Sierra Leoneans lost their lives, their innocence, and their child-hoods, some as victims, some as perpetrators. The trauma of this brutal war lingered with all those who remember it. Two of those include Aminata, who was abandoned during the war, and Joseph, who was orphaned by it. While the war was still raging, Saffie and Foday adopted Aminata and Joseph and provided a safe home for them amidst chaos and terror.

Devoted to her own immediate family as well as her village family, Saffie had been a tireless servant to her community and the many orphans created by Ebola, including seven children that she and Foday were caring for at the time in addition to their four biological daughters. Saffie had suffered hunger, battled malaria, and dealt with deep personal losses, but through it all, she persevered. She never lost her faith and her determination to thrive. She never stopped encouraging all those around her. That's why all people, women especially, flocked to Saffie due to her energy, confidence, and unwavering faith in God.

"When I am around Saffie, it is her strength, joy, and optimism, despite the tragedy she's faced, that stand out to me," Ben, the president of Just Hope, said, "She's a natural leader, as people are drawn to her grace, wisdom, and courage."

To see Saffie in 2016, you might have never known what an uncertain and frightening time she grew up in. When we met her, she was a pharmacist at the Baptist Eye Hospital, and was half-way through her four-year degree from Makeni University. Just in her early thirties, Saffie was a highly respected leader in Lunsar. She had also completed a seminary course offered in Lunsar and preached at local churches. She had planted several children's churches in the area, one of which was a fully constructed building under the leadership of the young adults who were once children Saffie gathered together under a pole and mud shelter.

We were proud to know Saffie and were grateful for her support of our efforts in Sierra Leone. We were reassured of Lunsar's future with determined and selfless people such as Saffie who led, inspired, and exemplified God's love.

Meeting other women like Saffie and having them share the full burden of their daily lives moved me. To experience firsthand the grace they exuded in the midst of such harsh circumstances didn't simply inspire me. It sustained me, especially during the dark season that began around this time.

TREADMILLS AND CROSSES

I had just finished being audited by the Commodity Futures Trading Commission (CFTC) when two people from the SEC showed up. The routine audit had gone fine; the CFTC did not find anything wrong with my bookkeeping or the way I traded. So naturally it was frustrating to hear that I was going to be audited again and had to produce

THE LAMB OF WALL STREET

yet again all the documents and forms I had just produced.

The frustration turned to shock when the SEC filed a case against me, accusing me of fraud. Then my shock became anger when I was forbidden to speak even in my own defense in an Atlanta courtroom.

When the long and drawn-out process was finally settled with the SEC in 2018, I lost the majority of my life savings. I was also told I could never be an accountant for the rest of my life. (I hadn't been an accountant for thirty years.) Like most people, I didn't have the resources to fight the SEC in court, so the settlement included a gag order they place on everybody that prevents me from challenging the truth of their allegations. There is little I can say about the facts in the case, but I can talk about my faith through the whole process.

Storms in life always shake your faith. Your beliefs will either be destroyed—or they will deepen. For me, the latter occurred, but only after someone walked alongside me and gave me the encouragement and advice I needed to move on.

During this process of battling for my reputation and respect with this matter with the SEC, I fell into a deep, dark hole, a place that I had never experienced before. I don't get depressed about anything; that's just not like me. This was different, however. My despondency wasn't just because of what was happening to me, but also what was happening to my investors.

I made an appointment to see one of my pastors, Lloyd. I went into Lloyd's office and explained to him what happened. I told him the details.

"Lloyd . . . I just—I can't function. I'm in a dark hole and I don't see how I'm going to get out of it."

My pastor could see and hear my desperation. He stood up and moved another chair in front of me and had it touching my knees. Then he walked back over to where he was sitting to face me.

"Karen, Jesus Christ is sitting in that chair," Lloyd said. "Talk to Him right now."

As I looked at the empty chair facing me, I started to weep. Lloyd walked over to his desk and picked up a box of tissue, then handed it to me.

"You talk to Jesus right now."

It took a few moments for me to collect myself, but when I began to talk, the words and emotions poured out of me.

It was one of the most amazing moments I've ever spent in my life.

I shared my anger and my hurt. The confusion and the frustration.

I never intended on being some kind of "super-trader." I never even knew I was going to be a trader. A free seminar suggested by my friend ended up changing my life. It ended up allowing me to do what I wanted to do, and that was running Just Hope and helping and empowering people all over the world.

God, you were leading me through that whole process. Without the trading, I would have never had the money to work with people all over the world.

I confessed my disbelief in what the SEC was doing and I shared my fears on what was going to happen next. I knew Jesus Christ was sitting in that chair listening to me. He heard every single word and saw every single emotion inside of me.

When I finished, I looked up at Lloyd.

Suyen, in Nicaragua.

The Kachimayu River in Peru.

A group of children who were living in a village in Sierra Leone.

A mother and child in Kroo Bay.

A true entrepreneur, she started cooking
food and selling it to the workers.

A typical African woman who lives in a village.

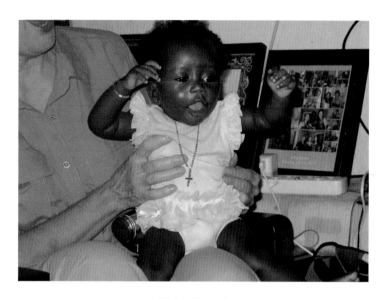

Baby Karen.

All children love to look at their picture.

Ben is crossing the river with local children.

Buying a coffin for Sautso was an emotional experience.

Everyone needs friends.

We are carrying chicks and guinea pigs
across the river to Anyana.

Blowing bubbles is the same everywhere.

Children are the same all over the world.

It was exciting to be breaking ground
for the pineapple plantation.

Elijah is a true artist.

It's wash day at the river.

Kroo Bay, Sierra Leone.

The Malawi solar-powered pumping station.

Striking water is as good as discovering gold!

La Chureca, Nicaragua.

The church in Perovo, Russia.

The village of Anyana, Peru.

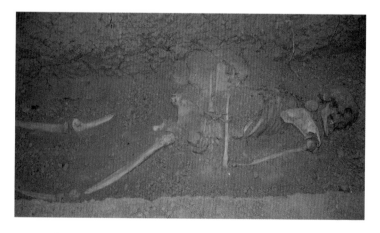

The museum in Ayacucho, which features displays
on what the Shining Path did to people.

This is my favorite African animal!

I am entering Kroo Bay.

Vincente writing in the book of remembrance in the museum.

We're getting dirt to make bricks.

One of the wells installed in Malawi by Just Hope.

Women walking to Sautso's burial site.

The witch doctor is dancing.

"Thank you so, so much," I said.

"We're not done," Lloyd said with a smile.

"Oh, really?"

"I want you to stand up," he told me. "Stand up, turn around, and sit in that chair."

I did what he asked, still confused by what he wanted.

"You are now sitting with Jesus Christ. Now, speak to Karen," Lloyd prayed.

I could feel the pain literally lifting off of me. I didn't hear some audible voice, but I could feel His words of hope covering and healing me.

This also was an amazing moment for me.

We don't have to see Pastor Lloyd and have him pull up a chair beside us to hear Christ speaking to us. His Spirit speaks to us through the Bible. So many verses give me strength for the day, like this one from Hebrews 12:3 (NIV): "Consider him who endured such opposition from sinners, so that you will not grow weary and lose heart."

Nothing I go through will ever match what Jesus went through for me. His words offer me a strength to keep going on.

Therefore lift your drooping hands and strengthen your weak knees, and make straight paths for your feet, so that what is lame may not be put out of joint but rather be healed. Strive for peace with everyone, and for the holiness without which no one will see the Lord. See to it that no one fails to obtain the grace of God; that no 'root of bitterness' springs up and causes trouble ... (Hebrews 12:12-15 ESV)

Bible verses like this can be powerful and painful in the same breath. Powerful in their wisdom and insight, yet painful when telling me what I should do.

I had to let go of a lot of the bitterness and anger I held inside.

The Sunday after my conversation with Pastor Lloyd, I had to drive to Atlanta so I packed early and knew I would miss church that day. The services are shown on their website later the following week. I was not pleased that I was going to miss church, but knew I had a long drive ahead of me. But when I got to the road where I should have turned left to get to the interstate, I turned right and went to church. I had no explanation for doing that. Lloyd walked out on the stage with a few men pushing a treadmill. They hooked it up, then Lloyd climbed on it and began walking just as he started his sermon. He didn't mention the treadmill or the fact that he was on it. He began his expository teaching and remained on the treadmill for thirty to forty minutes, sweating while he spoke to us.

At the end of his message, he stopped the machine and stepped off.

"Jesus Christ is telling us, 'Get off our treadmill.' "

As I sat in the pew, whatever bitterness and anger and resentment and hurt I held suddenly felt pushed up and out of me.

I haven't carried that burden with me since that day.

Sometimes when people ask me about what happened with the SEC, I get a little emotional thinking back on it. That burden has been taken off my heart and I was able to continue to live my life, yet that doesn't mean I am not reminded of the events every now and then. I have another remedy for this, and it's something I've been doing for many, many years.

I look for crosses.

They are everywhere to be found. I can see them while driving down the road, on telephone poles, and the sides of buildings. I see them in rooms and walls and ceilings. They are on smart phones and computer screens and commercials. I'm always looking for crosses, and they are constantly there.

Crosses are reminders that I will never go through the pain that Jesus Christ went through for me. I will never suffer like He suffered. Any stumbling block or difficult situation or hardship in my life only makes me stronger because it builds my relationship with God. All I have to do is remember what Christ did for me, and when I do, I have no room for complaining. None.

In some ways, I'm grateful for what I went through, because I'm so much closer to my Lord. I know He put his loving arms around me and took that pain off of me. It's almost crazy to say this, but I am almost grateful for what the SEC did to me because I would have just kept going with my regular life. Praying as always and going to church but not diving deeper in my relationship with Christ. The experience with the SEC brought me to a whole new level.

I never felt like Just Hope was all about me and my work. It was the Lord's work. It had grown into sites all over the world, not just in Sierra Leone. We were working with people in Honduras, Ghana, Togo, and Panama. We had a leader in Ben overseeing our efforts. Our work will continue regardless of what happens to me, and regardless of the name we are associated with.

One moment during the SEC crisis, Ben came to me and asked what needed to happen next.

"Let's do what needs to be done," I told him. "There're people to serve. Let's get on with it."

Getting on with it has always been my mantra and my mentality, whether it's been with my career or my ministry.

I love the quote at the start of this chapter that comes from Neil T. Anderson's book *The Daily*

Discipler: "Those who prosper in life know that endurance is the key to success." He goes on to say, "You will never fulfill your purpose in life if you continue to choose the path of least resistance or quit before you finish the race."[14]

The race is not about us, however. Anderson quotes Hebrews 10:36 (NIV) to give us a Biblical perspective on the race we are to run: "You need to persevere so that when you have done the will of God, you will receive what he has promised."

---

14 Neil T. Anderson, *The Daily Discipler* (Ada, MI: Bethany House, 2005).

*"I am fundamentally an optimist.
Whether that comes from nature or nurture,
I cannot say. Part of being optimistic
is keeping one's head pointed toward
the sun, one's feet moving forward."*

— NELSON MANDELA,

LONG WALK TO FREEDOM (1994)

Chapter Fifteen

DON'T GIVE
UP HOPE

DANCING AROUND THE BONFIRE

"What is your passion?"

So many years after Dr. J. Howard Olds asked me this question and set me out onto an unexpected journey, I asked myself this question again. This time, however, I knew the answer.

I want to help and encourage women in the countries we are serving in.

I recognized this passion of mine during a women's conference held primarily for the Baptist Pastors Wives Association of Sierra Leone, a group of about fifty women who traveled to Lunsar from all over the country. The conference theme was "Encouraging Women," and I had been asked to speak to the ladies who attended. Our goal with the conference was to empower women with technical agricultural ideas and business training. During one morning session centered around personal stories, I shared my own testimony since I was meeting these women for the first time. I knew if I opened up my heart, it would encourage women to do the same.

From the very first trip I took, I had witnessed how women were treated in different parts of the world. I will always remember walking down to the river with the women in Sierra Leone to fish, knowing whatever they caught would feed their children. If they didn't catch anything, they wouldn't eat. I saw firsthand how hard the women worked day after day. In some places, I would see women walking down the street behind their husbands. The men would have nothing in their hands while the women would be carrying everything.

Over the years, these women had become my heroes. At the conference I was able to share my appreciation for these women, many of whom were wives of pastors in the region. I was inspired by their hearts and their fortitude, and I realized just how isolated many of them are. Like all of us, these women needed a community and emotional support. The majority of groups working in underdeveloped communities around the world agree that women empowerment is the key to progress. As our work evolved in West Africa, we had become more intentional about engaging with women. In countries where being a widow can often mean being doomed to destitution, it is especially important that women have the means to take care of their families.

The women came to the conference from all over Sierra Leone, traveling by foot, motorcycles, or vehicles. We invited them to share their heaviest burdens with one another while also writing them down on slips of paper. The culture of the women in Sierra Leone was to keep their hurts and burdens to themselves, which resulted in feeling alone in their struggles.

The stories they tell revealed their struggles and pain, yet for every story we also heard songs of praise for God's love and faithfulness. In the face of death, rejection, and suffering, praise and thankfulness remained continually on their lips. The women sang, "Tell Him, tell Him, thank you, tell Papa God thank you."

After worshiping and praying together, we ventured outside for a time to give our burdens to the Lord and to lay them at the cross. We danced around a large bonfire and tossed our slips of paper that bore our burdens and pain into the flames as a symbol of releasing our cares and worries to the Lord. Isaiah 61:3 talks about this, about bestowing on them a crown of beauty instead of ashes, the oil of joy instead of mourning, and a garment of praise instead of a spirit of despair.

All of us walked away from this experience with a feeling of hope. Some carried this hope for the first time because they placed their hope in the one thing that truly lasts.

Hope is a beautiful and blessed thing. It's also a necessity. You can go forty days without food. We can all go seven days without water. Or seven minutes without air. But we cannot live a moment without hope. And from the very beginning, that's what I've been trying to do all over the world—to give people hope. Not through one person or one organization, but through one Savior.

WALKING AROUND THE RUINS

This is where the apostle Paul once stood.

I stood on a raised walkway amidst the relics of a former civilization that existed on the island of Cyprus. These were the ruins of the Basilica of Panagia Chrysopolitissa and the gothic church beside it that reside in the city of Paphos. The legend states that this was the place where the apostle Paul was tied down and beaten. I looked down at the remains of what they called St. Paul's Pillar, one of those pillars to which he was strapped as he was flogged. This was during the start of his ministry when he arrived at the island of Cyprus to preach about the good news of Jesus Christ as documented in Acts 13.

During that trip to Paphos, Paul, along with his companions Barnabus and John Mark, converted the Roman governor, Sergius Paulus, to Christianity. This was Paul's first missionary journey, the first of three documented journeys. Cyprus is the first country considered to have been governed by a Christian.

My heart was moved to be standing in this place.

This was the second time I'd visited Cyprus. The first time I came to this island, I came to visit a family whom I knew for about a week. I needed a break from everything happening back home— from the battle with the SEC and from the constant shadow it left over everything. I had been to Israel a couple of times, but this time I wanted to visit this island. I fell in love with it, and my spirit told me to come back here and stay. So that was what I decided to do.

I was focused on the thing I wanted to do for the rest of my life: helping women. I was moved to think of what the apostle Paul accomplished despite all his limitations and all the odds against him. Why couldn't I be bold like him and do the same?

Over time I studied where Paul went and saw firsthand the places he visited. Little by little I discovered the statistics of Christianity in Cyprus, learning that a low percentage of the people in Greece and Cyprus were Christians.

I need to do something about that, to reach out to other women, to share the gospel with them.

So I began on another journey, just like the one I had begun with Just Hope so many years ago. I didn't have a specific goal or a ten-year-plan. I just felt moved to do something in whatever way I could.

On my daily walks, I greeted the ladies I passed. I walked around three miles each day, passing beautiful houses and seeing women in their yards and on the sidewalks. Most of the women I met were British. Over time I began to get to know them.

"Hi, where are you from?" I asked them.

A greeting here, an introduction there. A conversation about Cyprus or America. Little by little, a relationship began. Little by little, I managed to get a group of ladies together. It took a year, and it went very slowly, but I just kept at it. Just like I have with everything for my entire life.

Little by little.

I lived on Cyprus for around two years, renting a wonderful three-bedroom villa with my backyard looking out to the Mediterranean Sea. The sun would sink into the sea every night. Every few months I left the island to go back to the U.S., and I spent time visiting places such as Greece, Turkey, Croatia, and Italy. But mostly I lived on Cyprus, getting to know other women.

These women, some of whom were local but the majority of whom were Brits living on Cyprus, were mostly what I considered agnostic. It wasn't that they didn't believe in God, but they never did anything about it. Once I knew these women well and knew they were comfortable with me, I suggested that we get together and do a Bible study. At first, I received shrugs and "Nahs," but I just kept talking about it.

"This will bring us together so we can spend social time with each other," I told them.

We eventually all came together and met as a group. There were twelve of us. Soon I suggested that we watch a DVD series called *The Armor of God* by Priscilla Shirer that equips women to be serious and strategic in their discipline of prayer. Priscilla Shirer is very relatable and can talk about any subject. I had taken the seven-session course with me to Cyprus.

The women responded with apathy to my idea. They didn't want to watch a set of DVDs. They weren't interested in that. But I asked them to simply watch one for me, and then I wouldn't make them watch anymore. After going through the first episode, it blew their minds. Naturally they wanted to see the rest of the series. It ended up having a strong impact on these women. Even when I finally left Cyprus in 2019, the women continued to meet together for Bible study.

In the midst of one of the darkest times of my life, I found purpose and peace. I found hope and happiness. God opened another door, an unlikely door, like He always has my entire life. Like so many others I came across, I didn't try to hand *out* the message of Jesus Christ to these women. Instead, I offered a hand *up* to them, and I did this by equipping them with Biblical principles and godly practices that allowed them to take control of their lives.

It's no different whether I'm in Nashville or Nicaragua. My goal remains the same in Cyprus or in South Africa.

I'm going to offer you a hand up, not a handout.

The key is trying to make an impact *that lasts.* To invest in people who want to help themselves. And always ask the big question related to: "Then what?"

It's a question we have to keep asking in our lives on a daily basis.

EPILOGUE

*T*he three lines in the opening epigraph of this book sum up my life in so many ways. They are from the well-known Robert Frost poem, "The Road Not Taken."

Everybody has moments in their lives where two roads will diverge, where they will have to make a choice which path to travel down. Years ago, I decided to take the road not taken, the one less traveled by, and yes . . . it *has* made all the difference. But it was a scary choice to take, and so many of us decide to keep on the familiar road we're on.

I sit here and think of everything I would have missed if I had stayed in corporate America and retired early. I thank God every day for allowing me to be used for His purposes. He didn't have to pick me. And I didn't have to pick the other road to walk down.

Overcoming our fears of walking through a door can bring overwhelming results. Vincente is an example of that.

On my second trip to Peru, the time where I experienced my big *aha* moment, Vincente and I were driving back to where I was staying and we passed through Ayacucho, a city in south-central Peru. I had heard about a museum there called Museo de la Memoria, which means Memory Museum. It is a museum in Ayacucho that is dedicated to the impact the Sendero Luminoso (Shining Path) had on Peru and the city that was most deeply affected by the conflict. The Museum of Memory was built between 2004 to 2005 and was the first for the victims impacted by the Shining Path.

The museum had only been open for a couple of years by the time we reached it. I asked Vincente if he would like to go in the museum, and he told me no but said he would be happy to take me there. When we arrived, he parked the car.

"I'm just going to sit here and wait on you," Vincente said.

I'll never forget stepping foot in Museo de la Memoria. This was the Peruvians' Holocaust. This museum was created and maintained by ANFASEP, the National Association of Relatives of the Kidnapped, Detained and Disappeared of Peru, and it serves as a reminder of the pain and courage shown in the people who have been affected. Inside you learn about historical events and see photos, last letters, and clothes that have been given by relatives of the victims.

The first exhibit I got to revealed a burial site where the Shining Path had buried people alive. Skeletal arms and feet were bound, meaning the people were probably put into a hole in the ground and then covered up by dirt, only to suffocate and die. After a few minutes of looking at this horrifying memorial, I was getting ready to walk out of the museum when Vincente showed up.

"So you've changed your mind about coming in here," I said.

"Yes. I would like to see this with you," Vincente told me.

So we walked through the three different rooms of the museum, stopping at each exhibit to study and stare at the images and information. We read about the history of ANFASEP shown through newspaper clippings, photographs, and items from the disappeared. Life-sized sculptures and ceramics depicted the violence.

At the very last exhibit, there was a newspaper article behind the glass. One showed a picture of a little boy and little girl, and the clipping told the story of how they were found dead. When Vincente saw this, he started to sob. I asked him what was wrong.

"This is my brother and sister," he said amidst his tears.

I've never cried that hard before in my life. We held each other and sank to our knees on the floor. Just holding each other and sobbing.

When we finally collected ourselves, we started walking out and passed a comment book in the museum. Vincente stopped and picked up the pen to start writing something. I never looked to see what he wrote down, nor did I ask him what he said.

I believe the experience of going through that museum provided some healing for Vincente with his grief. He was able to remember his missing brother and sister, and he was able to reflect on their lives. This museum was honoring their lives, and it moved Vincente and me just like it had moved so many others.

I'll never forget sharing that moment with Vincente. I'm glad he chose to get out of his car and enter the museum. I'm privileged to have walked beside him during those moments.

Vincente had chosen to take the path less traveled. This path took him to a place he didn't want to go, yet to a place he *needed* to go. A place he will never forget.

Some of us never go inside a museum to see what's inside; we're too afraid. Like I was about Africa. But then we go inside and find something miraculous awaiting us. Sometimes it can break our hearts, but it can also provide healing and strength.

It was 10:39 p.m. and I was finishing up work in my office. I was living in Cyprus and was used to starting to trade at four in the afternoon and finishing around eleven o'clock. I was really focused and getting ready to put an order in when I heard a voice inside of me. It was the same voice I heard that told me to leave my corporate job, the same voice that told me to let go of my animosity toward the SEC, the same voice that occasionally filled my spirit.

Tell your story now.

I didn't know how I would do that, but I knew I needed to tell my story. I never had an interest in sharing my story to the public, especially not in a book form. But I knew God wanted me to do this, to share my experiences with others, to let people know what He has done in my life. So I reached out to some people and started another journey that ultimately led to this book.

Everybody has a story to tell. Sometimes the story takes an unexpected turn, like mine did when I quit the corporate life to start a nonprofit. Sometimes there is more to the story, like in the case of Vincente. And sometimes, there are stories never told by others, ones we only learn about later after someone has passed away.

This happened with my father. The Associated Press headline in January 2020 describes what we learned: "WWII photos found in Salisbury tell story never spoken to family."

To say this was surprising is an understatement. I had found these pictures in my brother's house in Stanfield, North Carolina, after he passed away and traveled to Stanfield to clean his house.

My father was a very quiet man; personality wise, I'd say I take after his reserved spirit. I was so close to him, and after he passed away, it took me almost a year before I could even talk about it.

One subject James T. Bruton Jr. never spoke about was his time in the war. He was already working in Cannon Mills when World War 2 came along, and when he was drafted, he spent four years overseas. All I knew was that he went to Scotland and came down through Europe and Northern Africa. He had brought all this stuff home from the war, including boxes of pictures, but he stored them away and we never saw them. When my father died, my mother gave them to Larry, but the boxes remained unopened. It was only after my brother died that I found all of these items.

I decided to send a box of pictures to my brother's daughter, Deborah, who was the Fire Division Chief for Rowan County in North Carolina. I explained why I was giving them to her.

"If I take them, then one day I'll pass away and someone won't know what these pictures are."

Deborah started to go through the photos and discovered an old church envelope with surprising contents. She was quoted in the Associated Press article about what she found. "I was completely in shock. After being in the fire service for so long, I've seen some stuff, but I had never seen anything like that."

Inside the envelope were photos from a time in the war, and they showed images of dead bodies at a concentration camp. Emaciated bodies piled on top of one another. Right away Deborah sent the pictures to a historian, and after he went through all of them, he told her that these had been taken at Dachau concentration camp in Germany. They were taken on April 30, 1945, the day after the camp was liberated.

When Deborah told me what she had discovered, I fell to the ground and began to cry. I couldn't believe it. My emotions were both surprise and sadness.

My father was a hero. He never told us he was one of the men to rescue all these discarded lives in Dachau. I knew he was a quiet, spiritual man who would get on his knees at night and say a prayer. Little did I know the memories he carried with him.

"He wouldn't answer questions about it," I told the Associated Press. "I'm as surprised as anybody that he was in a German concentration camp. He never mentioned any part of what he did. I can't imagine him, being a humble Christian man, shooting people."[15]

My father died at a very young age of sixty-one and was buried in Salisbury at the National Cemetery. Now I understand why he passed away. He had to live with those memories. I'm glad we were able to send the photos to Dachau after the museum requested them in order to honor the victims and their families.

15 Associated Press, "WWII photos found in Salisbury tell story never spoken to family," 26 January 2020, https://statesville.com/townnews/military/wwii-photos-found-in-salisbury-tell-story-never-spoken-to-family/article_1bd91d8b-1f20-527f-9a86-540b3f372a2f.html (accessed 21 March 2021).

My father didn't share the pain and the horrors he had witnessed in World War II. Instead, he taught me about the important things in life. He showed me how to be independent and how to help people. He demonstrated what a life with humility looked like.

Now I realized he instilled in me my fearlessness to take on challenges and to help people all over the world, venturing into scary places just like he did.

Thinking of my father brings me back to my childhood once again, and to flying that kite. There's a lot you can learn from this simple exercise. A wise man once said, "Kites rise highest against the wind, not with it." And I have to say it's accurate—kites don't struggle when they face strong winds. They soar.

In a lot of ways, I've seen my life resembling a kite. I never believed I couldn't find a scholarship and enter the business world. I never accepted the notion I was meant to stay in Kannapolis and be paid less than others just because I was a woman. This resistance only forced me to work harder. The same goes for when I began to invest. I didn't give up. I could have given up. It would have been easy to give up. The same is true with my work with impoverished countries. The mistakes I made along the way and what the SEC did could have forced me to stop what I was doing. Those things have just strengthened my resolve and allowed me to hone in on what I want to accomplish.

The people who give up are not the people who are going to win the race. You have to stay with things. Not just your professional life, but your spiritual life. God wants you to stay in the race as it states in Hebrews 12:1 (NLT):

> *Therefore, since we are surrounded by such a huge crowd of witnesses to the life of faith, let us strip off every weight that slows us down, especially the sin that so easily trips us up. And let us run with endurance the race God has set before us.*

Sometimes it doesn't seem like you've run very far, but little by little, you can reach your destination. I still have places to go and still have goals to shoot for. God has given me a renewed focus and little by little, I plan to continue to make a difference in this world.